THE WORLD
AFTER GAZA

Also by Pankaj Mishra

THE WORLD AFTER GAZA

A History

PANKAJ MISHRA

PENGUIN PRESS

NEW YORK

2025

PENGUIN PRESS
An imprint of Penguin Random House LLC
1745 Broadway, New York, NY 10019
penguinrandomhouse.com

LIBRARY OF CONGRESS CONTROL NUMBER: 2024950722

ISBN 9798217058891 (hardcover)
ISBN 9798217058907 (ebook)

First published in Great Britain by Fern Press, an imprint of Vintage,
a division of Penguin Random House UK 2025

Printed in the United States of America
2 4 6 8 10 9 7 5 3 1

The authorized representative in the EU for product safety and compliance is
Penguin Random House Ireland, Morrison Chambers, 32 Nassau Street,
Dublin D02 YH68, Ireland. https://eu-contact.penguin.ie.

To PalFest and JVP, two beacons

We, too, are so dazzled by power and money that we forget the fragility of our existence: we forget that we are all in the ghetto, that the ghetto is fenced in, that outside the fence are the lords of death, and a little way off the train is waiting.

Primo Levi

If the solidarity of mankind is to be based on something more solid than the justified fear of man's demonic capabilities, if the new universal neighborship of all countries is to result in something more promising than a tremendous increase in mutual hatred and a somewhat universal irritability of everybody against everybody else, then a process of mutual understanding and progressing self-clarification on a gigantic scale must take place.

Hannah Arendt

Contents

Prologue

Think of the vast amount of brutality, cruelty and
lies which are able to spread over the civilized world.
Do you really believe that a handful of ambitious
and deluding men without conscience could have
succeeded in unleashing all these evil spirits if their
millions of followers did not share their guilt?

Sigmund Freud

On 19 April 1943, a few hundred young Jews in the
Warsaw Ghetto took up whatever arms they could find
and struck back at their Nazi persecutors. Most Jews in
the ghetto had already been deported to extermination
camps. The fighters were, as one of their leaders Marek
Edelman recalled, seeking to salvage some dignity: 'All
it was about, finally, was our not letting them slaughter
us when our turn came. It was only a choice as to the
manner of dying.'

After a few desperate weeks, the resisters were over-
whelmed. Most of them were killed. Some of those still
alive on the last day of the uprising committed suicide
in the command bunker as the Nazis pumped gas into

it; only a few managed to escape through sewer pipes. German soldiers then burned the ghetto, block by block, using flamethrowers to smoke out the survivors.

The Polish poet Czeslaw Milosz later recalled hearing screams from the ghetto 'on a beautiful quiet night, a country night in the outskirts of Warsaw':

> This screaming gave us goose pimples. They were the screams of thousands of people being murdered. It travelled through the silent spaces of the city from among a red glow of fires, under indifferent stars, into the benevolent silence of gardens in which plants laboriously emitted oxygen, the air was fragrant, and a man felt that it was good to be alive. There was something particularly cruel in this peace of the night, whose beauty and human crime struck the heart simultaneously. We did not look each other in the eye.

In a poem Milosz wrote in occupied Warsaw, 'Campo dei Fiori', he evokes the merry-go-round next to the ghetto's wall, on which riders move skyward through the smoke of corpses, and whose jaunty tune drowns out the cries of agony and despair. Living in Berkeley, California, while the US military bombed and killed hundreds of thousands of Vietnamese, an atrocity he compared to the crimes of Hitler and Stalin, Milosz again knew shameful complicity in extreme barbarity. 'If we are capable of compassion and at the same time are powerless,' he wrote, 'then we live in a state of desperate exasperation.'

Israel's annihilation of Gaza, provisioned by Western democracies, inflicted this psychic ordeal for months on millions of people – involuntary witnesses to an act of political evil, who allowed themselves to occasionally think that it was good to be alive, and then heard the screams of a mother watching her daughter burn to death in yet another school bombed by Israel.

The Shoah scarred several Jewish generations; Jewish Israelis in 1948 experienced the birth of their nation state as a matter of life and death, and then again in 1967 and 1973 amid annihilationist rhetoric from their Arab enemies. For many Jews who have grown up with the knowledge that the Jewish population of Europe was almost entirely wiped out, for no reason other than it was Jewish, the world cannot but appear fragile. Among them, the massacres and hostage-taking in Israel on 7 October 2023 by Hamas and other Palestinian groups rekindled a fear of another Holocaust.

But it was clear from the start that the most fanatical Israeli leadership in history would not shrink from exploiting an omnipresent sense of violation, bereavement and horror. Israel's leaders claimed the right to self-defence against Hamas, but as Omer Bartov, a major historian of the Holocaust, recognised in August 2024, they sought from the very beginning 'to make the entire

Gaza Strip uninhabitable, and to debilitate its population to such a degree that it would either die out or seek all possible options to flee the territory'. Thus, for months after 7 October, billions of people beheld an extraordinary onslaught on Gaza whose victims, as Blinne Ní Ghrálaigh, an Irish lawyer and South Africa's representative at the International Court of Justice in The Hague, put it, were 'broadcasting their own destruction in real time in the desperate, so far vain, hope that the world might do something'.

The world, or more specifically the West, didn't do anything. Behind the walls of the Warsaw Ghetto, Marek Edelman was 'terribly afraid' that 'nobody in the world would notice a thing', and 'nothing, no message about us, would ever make it out'. This wasn't the case in Gaza, where victims foretold their death on digital media hours before they were executed, and their murderers breezily broadcast their deeds on TikTok. Yet the livestreamed liquidation of Gaza was daily obfuscated, if not denied, by the instruments of the West's military and cultural hegemony: from the leaders of the United States and United Kingdom attacking the International Criminal Court and the International Court of Justice to the *New York Times* editors instructing their staff, in an internal memo, to avoid the terms 'refugee camps', 'occupied territory' and 'ethnic cleansing'.

Every day came to be poisoned by the awareness that while we went about our lives hundreds of ordinary people were being murdered, or being forced to witness the murder of their children. Pleas from people in Gaza, often well-known writers and journalists, warning that they and their loved ones were about to be killed, followed by news of their killing, compounded the humiliation of physical and political incapacity. Those driven by the guilt of helpless implication to scan Joe Biden's face for some sign of mercy, some sign of an end to bloodletting, found an eerily smooth hardness, broken only by a nervous smirk when he blurted out Israeli lies that Palestinians had beheaded Jewish babies. Righteous hopes aroused by this or that United Nations resolution, frantic appeals from humanitarian NGOs, strictures from jurors at The Hague, and the last-minute replacement of Biden as presidential candidate, were brutally dashed.

By late 2024, many people living very far from Gaza's killing fields were feeling – at a remove, but feeling – that they had been dragged through an epic landscape of misery and failure, anguish and exhaustion. This might seem an exaggerated emotional toll among mere onlookers. But then the shock and outrage provoked when Picasso unveiled *Guernica*, with its horses and humans screaming while being murdered from the sky, was the effect of a single image from Gaza of a father holding the headless corpse of his child.

The war will eventually recede into the past, and time may flatten its towering pile of horrors. But signs of the calamity will remain in Gaza for decades: in the injured bodies, the orphaned children, the rubble of its cities, the homeless peoples, and in the pervasive presence and consciousness of mass bereavement. And those who watched helplessly from afar the killing and maiming of tens of thousands on a narrow coastal strip, and witnessed, too, the applause or indifference of the powerful, will live with an inner wound, and a trauma that will not pass away for years.

The dispute over how to signify Israel's violence – legitimate self-defence, just war in tough urban conditions, or ethnic cleansing and crimes against humanity – will never be settled. It is not difficult to recognise, however, in the constellation of Israel's moral and legal infractions signs of the ultimate atrocity: the frank and routine resolves from Israeli leaders to eradicate Gaza; their implicit sanction by a public opinion deploring inadequate retribution by the IDF in Gaza; their identification of victims with irreconcilable evil; the fact that most victims were entirely innocent, many of them women and children; the scale of the devastation, proportionally greater than achieved by the Allied bombing of Germany in the Second World War; the pace of the killings, filling up mass graves across Gaza, and their modes, sinisterly impersonal (reliant on AI algorithms), and personal (snipers shooting children in the head, often twice); the denial of access to food and medicine; the hot metal sticks inserted into the rectum of naked prisoners; the destruction of schools, universities, museums, churches, mosques and even cemeteries;

the puerility of evil embodied by Israel Defense Forces soldiers dancing around in the lingerie of dead or fleeing Palestinian women; the popularity of such TikTok infotainment in Israel; and the careful execution of the journalists in Gaza documenting the annihilation of their own people.

Of course, the heartlessness accompanying an industrial-scale slaughter is not unprecedented. For decades now, the Shoah has set the standard of human evil. The extent to which people identify it as such and promise to do everything in their power to combat antisemitism serves, in the West, as the measure of their civilisation. But many consciences were perverted or deadened over the years European Jewry was obliterated. Much of Gentile Europe joined, often zealously, in the Nazi assault on Jews, and the news even of their mass murder was met with scepticism and indifference in the West, especially the United States. Reports of atrocities against Jews, George Orwell recorded as late as February 1944, 'bounce off consciences like peas off a steel helmet'. Western leaders declined to admit large number of Jewish refugees for years after the revelation of Nazi crimes. Afterwards, Jewish suffering was ignored and suppressed. Meanwhile, West Germany, though far from being de-Nazified, received cheap absolution from Western powers while being enlisted into the Cold War against Soviet communism.

These events which took place in living memory

undermined the basic assumption of both religious traditions and the secular Enlightenment: that human beings have a fundamentally 'moral' nature. The corrosive suspicion that they don't is now widespread. Many more people have closely witnessed death and mutilation, under regimes of callousness, timidity and censorship; they recognise with a shock that everything is possible, remembering past atrocities is no guarantee against repeating them in the present, and the foundations of international law and morality are not secure at all.

Much has happened in the world in recent years: natural catastrophes, financial breakdowns, political earthquakes, a global pandemic, and wars of conquest and vengeance. Yet no disaster compares to Gaza – nothing has left us with such an intolerable weight of grief, perplexity and bad conscience. Nothing has yielded so much shameful evidence of our lack of passion and indignation, narrowness of outlook and feebleness of thought. A whole generation of young people in the West was pushed into moral adulthood by the words and actions (and inaction) of its elders in politics and journalism, and forced to reckon, almost on its own, with acts of savagery aided by the world's richest and most powerful democracies.

Biden's stubborn malice and cruelty to the Palestinians was just one of many gruesome riddles presented by Western politicians and journalists. It would have been easy for Western leaders to withhold unconditional support to an extremist regime in Israel while also acknowledging the necessity of pursuing and bringing to justice those guilty of war crimes on 7 October. Why then did Biden repeatedly claim to have seen atrocity videos that do not exist? Why did Keir Starmer, a former human rights lawyer, assert that Israel has the right to 'withhold power and water' from Palestinians, and punish those in the Labour Party calling for a ceasefire? Why did Jürgen Habermas, the eloquent champion of the Western Enlightenment, leap to the defence of avowed ethnic cleansers? What made the *Atlantic*, one of the oldest periodicals in the United States, argue, after the murder of nearly eight thousand children in Gaza, that 'it is possible to kill children legally'? What explains the recourse to the passive voice in the mainstream Western media while reporting Israeli atrocities, which made it harder to see who is doing what to whom, and under what circumstances ('The lonely death of Gaza man with Down's syndrome' read the headline of a BBC report on Israeli soldiers unleashing an attack dog on a disabled Palestinian)? Why did American billionaires launch smear campaigns against protesters on college campuses, and help spur pitiless crackdowns on them? Why were academics and journalists sacked, artists and thinkers de-platformed, and young people barred from jobs, for appearing to defy a pro-Israel consensus? Why did the West, while defending and sheltering Ukrainians from a venomous assault, so pointedly exclude

Palestinians from the community of human obligation and responsibility?

The answers for many people around the world cannot but be tainted by a long-simmering racial bitterness. Palestine, as Orwell pointed out in 1945, is a 'colour issue'. This is the way it was inevitably seen by Gandhi, who, though sympathetic to the demand for a Jewish homeland, pleaded with Zionist leaders not to resort to terrorism against Arabs. Almost all post-colonial nations refused to recognise the State of Israel. India, China and Indonesia were among the countries that in 1975 passed a United Nations General Assembly Resolution declaring Zionism to be 'a form of racism and racial discrimination'. Unaddressed racial inequities weighed on Nelson Mandela when he said that South Africa's freedom from apartheid is 'incomplete without the freedom of the Palestinians'. They can still provoke the NAACP, the large and very mainstream American civil rights group, to make a rare intervention in foreign policy: it joined major African American church leaders in asking Biden to end military assistance to Israel.

For decades now, the racial divide on Palestine has been manifested most strikingly in black–Jewish relations in the United States. In US congressional primaries in 2024, interest groups affiliated with the American Israel Public Affairs Committee (AIPAC) spent more than $25 million to defeat the Democratic representatives Jamaal

Bowman and Cori Bush. The main transgression of these African American progressives in the eyes of their enemies was to have profaned what James Baldwin once called a 'pious silence' around Israel's behaviour. Baldwin himself had been bold enough to say that Israel, which sold arms to the apartheid regime in South Africa, embodied white supremacy and not democracy. He also pointed out, in 1967, that the suffering of the Jewish people 'is recognised as part of the moral history of the world' and 'this is not true for the blacks'. 'Black history has been blasted, maligned, and despised,' he charged. 'The Jew is a white man, and when white men rise up against oppression, they are heroes: when black men rise, they have reverted to their native savagery. The uprising in the Warsaw ghetto was not described as a riot, nor were the participants maligned as hoodlums.'

Baldwin abridged a long historical experience: the Jew is not a white man in any simple sense, and was hardly seen as such by other white men. Much of Israel's population consists of Jews of Middle Eastern ancestry. Yet in 2024 many more people conflate it with white-majority (and majoritarian) Western nations. Billions of non-Westerners have been furiously politicised in recent years by the West's calamitous war on terror, which demonstrated, through the despoiling of large parts of South Asia, the Middle East and North Africa, killings by drones, and a gulag in the Caribbean, the ease with which black and brown bodies could be seized, broken and destroyed outside all norms and laws of war. In their eyes, the Western denial of technology to poor countries to make their own antidotes to Covid-19, and the hoarding of vaccines past their sell-by date – what came to be termed 'vaccine apartheid' – confirmed yet again that the West seeks always to protect its own interests under the guise of a universalist rhetoric of democracy and human rights. They see the garish discrepancy between the West's generous hospitality to Ukrainian refugees and the barriers it builds to keep out darker-skinned victims of its own failed wars.

They can see, too, that, when compared with the Jewish victims of Nazism, the numerous late-Victorian holocausts in Asia and Africa, and the nuclear assaults on Hiroshima and Nagasaki are barely remembered in the West. They can hardly fail to notice a belligerent version of 'Holocaust denial' among the elites of former imperialist countries, who refuse to address their countries' past of genocidal brutality and plunder and try hard to delegitimise any discussion of this as unhinged 'wokeness'. Popular West-is-best chronicles of the modern world continue to ignore the acute descriptions of Nazism (by Jawaharlal Nehru, George Padmore and Aimé Césaire, among other imperial subjects) as the 'twin' of Western imperialism; they shy away from exploring the obvious connection between the imperial slaughter of natives in the colonies and the genocidal terrors perpetrated against Jews inside Europe.

*

In 1967 the Iranian thinker Ali Shariati expressed an argument of the 'darker peoples' that has not changed for decades:

> Why should the West and Christianity give up Islamic Palestine as payoff? Why shouldn't they give up a part of Poland where they put the Jews under the most terrible torture? Why don't they give one state of the Federal Republic of Germany as compensation for the Holocaust? Why should Christianity compensate for its torture of the Jews during the past two-thousand years from the pocket of Islam? Why should the West pay for its crimes from the empty pockets of the Middle East nations?

In this respect, and many others, the conflict between Israel and Palestine is not equal to the many other conflicts for independence, territory and sovereignty, of the kind seen in Kashmir, Cyprus, East Timor and the Balkans. Supporters of Israel claim that the critics worldwide of the 'Middle East's only democracy' are hypocritically and sinisterly obsessed with its treatment of Palestinians, while remaining indifferent to Russia's atrocities in Ukraine, the persecution of Uighur Muslims in China, and mass killings and displacement in Syria, Sudan and the Congo. But Israel is a focus of world events not only because it hosts the holy sites of three major religions, is located at one of the most sensitive points in the global networks of geopolitical and financial power, and, unlike Russia, China, Syria, Sudan and the Congo, receives seemingly limitless moral and material assistance from Europe and the United States. It is also because the actions of a Jewish state in the Middle East originally formed to solve a Western problem – the Jewish question – implicate, and divide, much of humanity.

The formation of Israel by European Jews in the Middle East just as Europe retreated from Asia and Africa was always going to have greater significance than the creation of any other new state. Decolonisation is the central event of the twentieth century for an overwhelming majority of the human population. Realising a millenarian dream in Palestine just as Asians and Africans liberated themselves from European colonialism almost guaranteed that normalisation, the ardent desire of European Zionists, would not be achieved; that the most dramatic century in Jewish history would continue; and Jews in Israel and the diaspora would remain as both objects and agents at the very heart of the modern world's vast and fateful confrontations: if no longer between religious tradition and secular modernity, capitalism and socialism, democracy and totalitarianism, then between Arabs and Jews, Global North and Global South, and white and non-white peoples.

Today, the seemingly undefusable antagonism between Israelis and Palestinians is mapped on one of the most treacherous fault lines of modern history: the 'colour line', described by W. E. B. Du Bois as the central problem of international politics, defined by the extent to which racial difference is 'made the basis of denying to over half the world the right of sharing to their utmost ability the opportunities and privileges of modern civilization'. The danger of a conflagration erupting in the Middle East and consuming much of the world cannot be overstated. The ideological hostilities are already rending the social fabric of several societies. In the sharper international alignment after Gaza and Lebanon, many Jews world-wide find themselves confronting another, much larger group of people also claiming to be victims of the geno-cidal racism of Western countries. A global civil society once seemed possible around the transvaluation of the Shoah as the ultimate atrocity and antisemitism as the nastiest form of bigotry. Other groups now advance rival claims, attesting to historical mass crimes of genocide, slavery and racist imperialism, and demanding recogni-tion and reparation.

They are prone to ask: has the Western focus on the crimes of Nazi and communist totalitarianism deliber-ately obscured closer examination of the West's original sin of white supremacy? New forms of antisemitism have emerged around the world, but what explains the belligerent new forms of philosemitism within those Western countries that once deemed the Jewish popula-tion to be alien and indigestible and extirpated most of it? Exploring this transformation is hardly an academic exercise as the far right surges across the West, blurring its self-image as exemplar of liberal democracy to the world, and historically antisemitic white nationalists, from Hungary's Viktor Orbán to American evangelicals, fervently join the defence of Israel.

There are many other disquietingly unexplored issues. Has the Americanisation of the Shoah distorted its history, and corrupted the foreign policies of the United States and its European allies? The Jewish imperative to remember the Shoah has spawned several derivations in Western societies, all aiming for the same moral prestige and advantage of victimhood. Are the narratives of suffering derived from the Shoah, slavery and colonialism destined to clash, or can they be reconciled? The 'struggle of man against power', Milan Kundera famously said, 'is the struggle of memory against forgetting'. But when does organised remembrance become a handmaiden to brute power, and a legitimiser of violence and injustice?

The following pages try to address these questions. But they aim most of all to frame them sufficiently precisely, so we can at least look squarely at the phenomenon we confront: a catastrophe jointly inflicted by Western democracies, which has destroyed the necessary illusion that emerged after the defeat of fascism in 1945 of a common humanity underpinned by respect for human rights and a minimum of legal and political norms.

The orgy of killing that began on 7 October 2023 and continued for many months and in several countries has ruptured time and removed the world before Gaza to another era; and I am conscious of writing in a strange chasm, between an insufficiently understood past and a menacing future, whose most sinister signs must be quickly identified. This book is not, and cannot be, a detached account of the origins and impact of the defining event of the twenty-first century. Though dependent on scholarly works for illumination, its self-made paths describe a personal intellectual journey.

I grew up in India imbibing the reverential Zionism of my family of Brahmin Hindu nationalists. Lack of personal familiarity with Jewish people, or knowledge of Israel, was no obstacle to our admiration for Zionism. The first Jew I knew of was an Indian writer in Bombay: Nissim Ezekiel, a pioneering modernist, whose poem 'The Night of the Scorpion' was required reading for schoolchildren across India. The second was a historical figure, David Sassoon, the Arabic-speaking pre-eminent businessman of nineteenth-century Bombay, who had left a rich cultural and architectural legacy in the city. The presence of Ezekiel in Bombay, among one of Asia's ancient Jewish communities, together with the statues, library, schools, docks connected to the Sassoons, a Jewish family from Baghdad, gave me a strong early impression that the Jews were a Westernised but fundamentally Asian minority, like the Parsis of Persian origin.* In pictures we possessed of Albert Einstein and Rabindranath Tagore sitting side by side, the two friends looked like Oriental sages.

Later readings in history and literature dispelled these childish visions, and alerted me to the injustice suffered by Palestinians. A visit to the West Bank in 2008 finally jolted me out of a languid view of Zionism as vindication and shield of the eternally persecuted, and into a deeper understanding of the long Palestinian ordeal. At the same time, I found it increasingly difficult to communicate that understanding.

Memories of Jewish suffering at the hands of the Nazis were, I recognised, the foundation on which many post-1945 descriptions of extreme ideology and atrocity, and most demands for recognition and reparations, had been built. I came to see how the Shoah had become a universal standard for gauging the political and moral health of societies. I myself deployed this influential measure in my writings in Western periodicals about the Hindu nationalist admirers of Hitler and their malign influence over India. I often cited the Jewish experience of prejudice to warn against the barbarism that becomes possible when certain taboos are broken.

But my Indian background and engagement with

---

* An impression strengthened by the fact that Zubin Mehta, the world's most famous Parsi, was the music director of the Israel Philharmonic Orchestra.

non-Western societies also made for a different emphasis: they predisposed me to look at Europe's mid-twentieth-century racial apocalypse alongside rather than separate from other atrocities suffered by minorities and colonised peoples in the modern era. Zionism, too, appeared to me in a different light, inextricable from redemptive projects of humiliated peoples in Asia and Africa, in both its early motivations and later mutations. A heightening experience of Hindu nationalism through the 1990s and 2000s made me understand better how collective memory was manipulated by ideological movements and how their violent expansion and siege mentalities come to be mutually intensifying.

In sporadic attempts to tackle the subject of Palestine from this vantage point outside the West and the Middle East, I become more aware of an insidious Western regimen of repressions and prohibitions. Palestinians and Arabs have known for decades the many hidden red lines constraining discussion of Israel's trajectory; the evidence they offered of the abuse of the Shoah's memory by Israel's leaders, antisemitic politicians and Islamophobic agitators was long ago deemed unwelcome. But it wasn't just their perspectives that were suppressed or unheeded. Western ruling classes, as has become clearer lately, seemed to have decreed a broader proscription while trying to insulate Israel from criticism.

This intellectual despotism at a range of institutions – from museums, universities and publishers to corporate headquarters, banks and non-profits – turned more punitive as the blithe slaughter of innocents in Gaza accelerated.* I felt almost compelled to write this book, to alleviate my demoralising perplexity before an extensive moral breakdown, and to invite general readers into a quest for clarifications that feel more pressing in a dark time.

I was driven, too, by a deeper personal motivation. Judging different kinds of post-war moral responsibility in 1945, the philosopher Karl Jaspers spoke of 'metaphysical guilt' – the affliction of those who become impotently aware of inconceivable barbarism in their midst. 'There exists,' Jaspers said, 'a solidarity among men as human beings that makes each co-responsible for every wrong and injustice in the world, especially for crimes committed in his presence or with his knowledge. If I fail to do whatever I can to prevent them, I too am guilty.'

I write out of that guilt – a broad human condition after Israel's livestreamed mass-murder spree in the Middle East – and the obligation that the living have to the innocent dead. I also write with the faith that there is such a thing as solidarity between human beings as human beings, and it does not end at the colour line.

* The lecture on which this book is partly based was pre-emptively cancelled by its London hosts, the Barbican Centre. I also had to give up my decade-long column on current affairs at Bloomberg.

Part One

AFTERLIVES
OF THE SHOAH

Israel and the Incurable Offence

In survival, each man is the enemy of every other,
and all grief is insignificant measured against
this elemental triumph. Whether the survivor is
confronted by one dead man or by many, the essence
of the situation is that he feels *unique*.

Elias Canetti

In 1977, a year before he killed himself, the Austrian
writer Jean Améry came across press reports of the
systematic torture of Arab prisoners in Israeli prisons.
Arrested in Belgium in 1943 while distributing anti-Nazi
pamphlets, Améry himself had been brutally tortured
by the Gestapo before being deported to Auschwitz.
He managed to survive, and though he refrained from
writing about them for two decades he could never look
at his torments as things of the past. He insisted that
'whoever has succumbed to torture can no longer feel
at home in the world. The shame of destruction cannot
be erased. Trust in the world, which already collapsed in
part at the first blow, but in the end, under torture, fully,
will not be regained.' Twenty-two years later, Améry

wrote, 'I am still dangling over the ground by dislocated arms.'

Profoundly disturbed by reports of torture in Israel and 'sonorous but not entirely convincing' denials from Israelis, he immediately wrote an article titled 'The Limits of Solidarity'. Améry, the son of a Jewish father and Catholic mother, had grown up in Austria with no connection to Judaism. Nor had he been sympathetic to any of the main currents of Zionism. The belief that Jews constitute a nation with the right to collective self-determination had flourished initially among secular German-speaking Jews such as Theodor Herzl and Max Nordau, and was pursued in Palestine by Jewish immigrants from Europe. The utopia of a 'Jewish homeland' came to be imagined diversely: a refuge from antisemitism and arbitrary despots, in Uganda as well as Poland, or a place where Jewish religion and culture could flourish. In 1917, political Zionists managed to secure from Britain a declaration – later called the Balfour Declaration – that supported the creation in Palestine of a Jewish 'national home'. Until the 1930s, however, only a tiny minority of European Jews pursued the idea of returning to the Zion of the biblical imagination.

It was the unrelentingly ferocious antisemitism of the 1930s, enshrined in racial laws, that forced Améry, and many other assimilated German Jews, to first reckon with his own identity. 'For me,' he wrote, 'being Jewish equates to feeling the burden of yesterday's tragedy within oneself. I bear the number from Auschwitz on my left forearm.' Then, like many survivors of Nazi death camps, those with memories of barbed wire, skeletal figures, beatings, stony-faced Germans with large vicious dogs shouting humiliating orders, pits of death, and endless smoke from chimneys, Améry had come to feel an 'existential connection' to Israel.

After 1945, when only three million of Europe's nine and a half million Jews looked to have survived Hitler's 'Final Solution', the many different visions of a Jewish homeland since the nineteenth century narrowed into an urgency to gather Jews from throughout the world in Palestine, and to ensure their safety. With much of the West barred to Jewish survivors, European animus against Jews showed few signs of diminishing.

Moreover, Western countries quickly forgave, even embraced, culpable Germans after 1945. Living in Austria and Germany, 'where the Nazi war criminals are either not prosecuted at all or receive laughably short prison sentences, of which they serve barely a third anyway', deepened the 'extreme *loneliness*' Améry had known in front of his German torturers. 'I have been unable,' he confessed, 'to trouble yesterday's murderers and tomorrow's potential aggressors with the moral truth of their misdeeds because the world as a whole did not assist me in doing so. Hence, I am as alone as I was when I was being tortured.'

Israel seemed the only refuge for, in Améry's words,

'all the humiliated and libeled Jews the world over'. Yet, established through war and ethnic cleansing, and surrounded by dispossessed peoples and vengeful nations, Israel turned out to be no place of safety, where Jewish existence could be, as Zionists originally hoped, finally 'normalized'. In 1966, Améry wrote that 'the demand of some Arab statesman that Israel be wiped off the map cuts me to the quick'. Améry became extremely sensitive to events – the Palestinian murder of Israeli athletes at the Munich Olympics of 1972, the Yom Kippur War of 1973, in which a coalition of Arab states attacked Israel – that seemed to threaten the hard-won security of a viciously persecuted people. He was particularly angered and alienated by condemnations of Israel as a racist colonialist power by the young Western leftists he considered his political allies.

Jews had been prominent figures in the Western internationalist left that emerged after the Russian Revolution and distinguished itself through a valiant if losing battle against fascism in Spain. Socialism offered Jews not only integration and acceptance within their societies but also a likely role in shaping their future. Thus, Jews came to be represented disproportionately in left-wing parties, notably in Soviet Russia – so much so that Jewishness came to seem, to lethal effect in the eyes of Nazis and Ukrainian and Polish nationalists, a cosmopolitan bulwark against the ethnically defined community. Early

Zionist settlers from Europe brought with them to Palestine socialistic ideas of collective farming, trade unions and economic planning. Inheriting some of their virtuous aura, the first Jewish state generated a range of blurry first impressions.

In 1947, Stalin crucially supported, together with the Soviet Union's satellite states – Belorussia, Ukraine, Poland and Czechoslovakia – and Communist parties in Britain and Italy, the United Nations' plan for partitioning Palestine and creating a Jewish state. Acting through Czech intermediaries, the Soviet Union also armed the Zionists, who subsequently led or enabled the expulsion of approximately 750,000 Palestinians – the ethnic cleansing of Palestine in 1948 that founded Israel and is remembered by Palestinians as the Nakba. The radical American journalist I. F. Stone famously compared Israeli Jews during the state's founding to 'the men of Concord or Lexington'. While admitting in 1967 that 'Israel is an ally of the United States' and 'a pawn of imperialism' and that 'this is embarrassing', the Italian writer Primo Levi still insisted that 'Israel came into being precisely to serve an anti-imperialist function, exploiting and hastening the collapse of British colonialism' and 'the Israeli constitution seems to me solidly constructed on a socialist and democratic base'.

A range of prominent Western intellectuals and activists, from Jean-Paul Sartre, Améry's own hero, to the influential American theologian Reinhold Niebuhr and Martin Luther King, took a similarly benevolent view of Israel as an egalitarian refuge for a pitilessly abused people. The sympathy for Israel was helped at least partly by a reflexive contempt for Arabs among the Western intelligentsia. In a letter to Hannah Arendt in 1959 from Libya, Mary McCarthy evoked stereotypes of ragged, illiterate and gesticulating natives, writing that 'the Arabs, except when they form a picture out of Italian painting, seem odious and unattractive'. Reporting on Palestinian refugees in 1961, the celebrated foreign correspondent Martha Gellhorn wrote, 'Arabs gorge on hate, they roll in it, they breathe it.'

But, as decolonisation accelerated in Asia and Africa, and Western powers launched neocolonial wars in Africa and Indochina, many in a younger generation of left-wingers started to affiliate themselves to the formerly colonised peoples of the Third World. Members of the so-called New Left in Germany in particular were disgusted by the unexamined Nazi past of their elders, and angered, too, as the US military devastated Vietnam, by what they saw as the dominance of unrepentant white supremacists in Western Europe and the United States. New Leftists sought hope and inspiration from the quasi-socialist national independence movements in Asia and Africa and the Caribbean. They took to denouncing Israel as a racist colonialist enterprise after the Six Day War in 1967, when Israel briskly conquered the Golan Heights, the West Bank of the Jordan River, East Jerusalem, the Gaza Strip and the Sinai Peninsula.

For many people with Améry's socialist sympathies, Israel's ostracism by erstwhile and potential comrades came as a shock. He attacked young left-wing critics of the Jewish state as 'thoughtless and unscrupulous'; he may have been one of the first to make the claim, habitually amplified now by Israel's leaders and supporters, that virulent antisemites disguise themselves as virtuous anti-imperialists and anti-Zionists. He became more despondent with the left after the Yom Kippur War in 1973, when Israel seemed weaker and more isolated than ever. He despairingly noted the alliance between German far-leftists and Palestinian militants when in 1976 they jointly hijacked an Air France flight with 248 passengers, diverting it to Entebbe in Uganda, where the kidnappers separated Israelis from non-Israelis.* Yet the 'admittedly ambiguous and sketchy' reports of torture in Israeli prisons prompted Améry to consider the limits of his solidarity with Israel.

---

* Améry may have known that a Shoah survivor among the Jewish hostages showed one of the German kidnappers the number tattooed on his arm and said to him in German: 'I was mistaken when I told my children that there is a different Germany . . . I see that nothing has changed in Germany.' In reply, the German militant blamed the German establishment for embracing Nazis, adding, 'My friends and I are here to help the Palestinians, because they are the underdog. They are the ones suffering.'

He began what turned out to be one of his last essays, published in *Die Zeit*, one of Germany's leading weeklies, by warning of another war between Israel and Arab countries, and the possibility that 'one day the immense economic, military, and potential technological advantage of the Arabs' would result in 'a catastrophe on a par with Auschwitz'. He spoke yet again of 'burgeoning antisemitism'. He went on to criticise the trend to ultra-Zionism in Israel, and worried that the country would lose the support of Jews in the diaspora. He exhorted Israel to 'treat the terrorists who oppose you and who have long since transgressed the bounds of morality with a measure of humanity'. He emphasised that he shared the 'anguish of every victim of torture, even if he is an Arab terrorist with blood on his hands'. 'I urgently call on all Jews who want to be human beings,' he said, 'to join me in the radical condemnation of systematic torture. Where barbarism begins, even existential commitments must end.'

Améry killed himself a few months later. 'I am a man of 65 years,' he wrote in his last year, 'more perplexed now than I was as a twenty-year-old youth.' For Shoah survivors, the first three decades after 1945 had been exceptionally bleak. All surviving Nazis, apart from the most monstrous war criminals, had gone unpunished or enjoyed lenient sentences. In Améry's own bitter words: 'The generation of the destroyers – the gas chamber constructors, those ready at any time to sign their name to anything, the generals duty-bound to their Fuhrer – is growing old with honor.' But lack of scruple was also becoming evident in the state ostensibly built to house the victims of the Shoah. Among Améry's perplexities was the apotheosis of Menachem Begin as Israel's prime minister in 1977 – an event that scandalised many who had seen Israel as a small left-leaning country fighting for its life.

Begin belonged to the 'Revisionist' tradition of Zionism founded by Vladimir Jabotinsky soon after the Balfour Declaration in 1917, in which Jewish youth wearing military uniforms and performing martial drills in Eastern Europe envisioned the Jewish state as militantly uncompromising, with no concessions to Palestinian Arabs or the neighbouring Arab states. Since 1977, most Israeli governments have been dominated by the Likud, Begin's political party and Revisionism's political heir. Benjamin Netanyahu, the country's longest-serving prime minister, is the son of one of Revisionism's leading publicists, Benzion Netanyahu, who served as a secretary to Jabotinsky. For decades, however, the Revisionists were ruthlessly stigmatised by their left-leaning rivals in both the pre-state Jewish community in Palestine, the Yishuv, and the State of Israel.

David Ben-Gurion, Israel's first prime minister, called Jabotinsky 'Vladimir Hitler' at a public rally in Tel Aviv in 1933. Begin, who revered Jabotinsky as 'our immortal teacher and leader', himself invited such descriptions after he organised, during the Zionist campaign against the British in Palestine, the 1946 bombing of the King David Hotel in Jerusalem in which ninety-one people were killed. In 1948, Zionist militias, including a group commanded by Begin, massacred more than a hundred Arab civilians in the village of Deir Yassin, one of the grislier events of the Nakba.

Visiting the United States a few months later, Begin found himself and his cohorts pointedly compared to Nazis and fascists in a joint letter to the *New York Times* signed by, among others, Hannah Arendt and Albert Einstein. 'The public avowals of Begin's party,' the letter claimed, 'are no guide whatever to its actual character. Today they speak of freedom, democracy and anti-imperialism, whereas until recently they openly preached the doctrine of the Fascist state. It is in its actions that the terrorist party betrays its real character; from its past actions we can judge what it may be expected to do in the future.'

The letter ended presciently with a warning: 'It is all the more tragic that the top leadership of American Zionism has refused to campaign against Begin's efforts, or even to expose to its own constituents the dangers to Israel from support to Begin.' By 1977, however, Begin had settled, with the help of American Zionists, into the mainstream of Israeli politics, along with the Gush Emunim – literally 'Block of the Faithful' – a millenarian

Jewish supremacist group committed to taking permanent possession of occupied Palestinian land.

This was nothing less than a moral and political revolution. In retrospect, Begin's victory in 1977 seems a culmination of Israel's second founding during the Six Day War in 1967, when, occupying Arab lands, the country reaffirmed itself as an expansionist power. The national mood changed from pessimism to euphoria as Israel became Goliath rather than David, support for an apparently powerful Jewish state surged among Jewish Americans, and left-leaning Zionist politicians like Shimon Peres as well as Begin and Ariel Sharon began to sustain the project of building Jewish settlements in the occupied territories – 'facts on the ground', in Israeli parlance, that rendered impossible a sovereign Palestinian state.

Once condemned as 'Hitlerite' by his rival Ben-Gurion, Begin now confidently hurled the same accusation at Palestinian leaders. He attacked the 'gentiles' who failed to support Jews before and during the Shoah, and took to routinely invoking the Holocaust and the Bible while assaulting Arabs and building settlements. In 1981 German Chancellor Helmut Schmidt suggested that Germany had a moral commitment to the Palestinians since the latter had suffered injustice upon the establishment of the State of Israel; Begin responded by accusing Schmidt of participating in the Shoah, and asked him to get down on his knees and apologise.

These remarks did not come out of the blue. They represented a deepening fixation with the Shoah in official Israeli rhetoric, and a radical re-envisioning of Israel's identity and purpose: as a country that would forever be on guard against another Shoah, while redeeming with its military power the millions of Jews who had remained in the European diaspora and gone unresistingly to their death.

After 7 October 2023, when Palestinian militants murdered more than a thousand Israelis, Israel's politicians repeatedly brought up the killing of six million Jews in Europe. Israeli diplomats at the UN wore yellow Star of David patches, and Netanyahu compared children cowering as Hamas gunmen rampaged through kibbutzim to Anne Frank. However, during Israel's early years, when its socialistic idealism attracted the admiration of Western leftists, the Shoah was not an intense national preoccupation. Rather, the state had a profoundly ambivalent and often manipulative relationship with the Shoah's European victims.

In his 2004 book *In the Shadow of the Holocaust*, Yosef Grodzinsky describes the narrow Zionist-centric view of David Ben-Gurion, who was exasperated by the great majority of diaspora Jews who refused to become Zionists and move to Palestine to contribute to his nation-building project. This need was manifest in his notorious remark in 1938: 'if I knew it was possible to save all children of Germany by their transfer to

England and only half of them by transferring them to the Land of Israel, I would choose the latter, because we are faced not only with the accounting of these children but also with the historical accounting of the Jewish people'.

Seeing Zionism as a 'rejection of the Diaspora they loathed', the Israeli historian Tom Segev writes in *The Seventh Million* (1993), Israeli leaders radiated 'arrogance and contempt towards the Holocaust's victims and survivors'. Ben-Gurion, like other Israeli leaders at the time, initially saw Shoah survivors as 'human debris'. Claiming that they had survived only because they had been 'harsh, evil, egotistic', he did not regard them as fit human material for the urgent task of building a strong Jewish state. Ben-Gurion had an even lower opinion of the Jewish immigrants from Arab countries who substituted for the murdered Jews of Europe, and who, though soon constituting the country's majority population, faced racist discrimination from the country's Ashkenazi ruling class of European ancestry.

All this changed with Begin, and more rapidly after Adolf Eichmann, the SS officer in charge of transporting European Jewry to the death camps, was put on trial in Israel in 1961. A survivor of the Shoah from Poland, Begin saw a political opportunity in Israel's hastily and imperfectly imagined community: it was he who turned the murder of six million Jews into a new basis for Israel's identity, especially among the ill-treated and resentful Jewish voters of Middle Eastern origin, the Mizrahim. It was also under Begin that the Israeli establishment began to produce and disseminate the very particular version of the Shoah – as imminent danger – that Israel's leaders still use today to legitimise their routine expansionism and bouts of spectacularly disproportionate violence against Palestinians.

Améry recognised early the likely consequences of Israel's transformation for Jews living outside Israel. That Begin, 'with the Torah in his arm and taking recourse to biblical promises', speaks openly of stealing Palestinian land 'alone would be reason enough', he wrote, 'for the Jews in the diaspora to review their relationship to Israel'. Shortly before he committed suicide, Améry pleaded with Israelis to 'acknowledge that your freedom can be achieved only with your Palestinian cousin, not against him'.

Many other Shoah survivors took a more categorical view of developments in Israel. Marek Edelman, one of the commanders of the Warsaw Ghetto uprising in 1943, and a leading figure in Poland's Solidarity movement, denounced what he called the 'Israeli philosophy, which consists of believing that you can kill 20 Arabs as long as one Jew remains alive'. 'Jews in the Near East,' Jurek Becker, one of the very few Jewish novelists in post-1945 Germany, wrote in 1977, 'have established themselves as a master race and are practising a kind of politics that I can only describe as predatory.'

Anxieties about Israel's lurch to the right exploded in the public sphere when, in June 1982, Begin, insisting that Arabs were the new Nazis and Yasser Arafat the new Hitler, launched an assault on Palestinian refugees in Lebanon. In the war's most infamous episode, Lebanese Christian militiamen allied with Israel entered two refugee camps and over several days shot and hacked to death hundreds of men, women and children; the 81mm mortars of the Israel Defense Forces (IDF) firing illumination rounds lit up the skies at night to facilitate the massacre. The French writer Jean Genet, one of the first Europeans to enter the camps, recorded how 'from one wall of the street to the other, bent or arched, with their feet pushing against one wall and their heads pressing against the other, the black and bloated corpses that I had to step over were all Palestinian and Lebanese'.

US president Ronald Reagan had already accused Begin of perpetrating a 'Holocaust' and ordered him to end it. Faced with greater international outcry after the slaughter of refugees, Begin accused his critics of levelling a 'blood libel' against Israel and the Israel Defense Forces. But the facts were incontrovertible: the IDF had killed thousands of Palestinians and Lebanese and obliterated large parts of Beirut.

Günther Anders, the Viennese writer (and Hannah Arendt's first husband), published an open letter renouncing his membership of the local Jewish community. 'What Begin has just done,' he charged, 'goes beyond what could be defended as "retaliation" or "self-defence": he has managed to make me, who hates self-hatred, blush at the idea of belonging to this people.' The 'Israeli people', Anders added, had obeyed Begin 'as blindly as the German people obeyed Hitler when he exterminated six million of us'.

Primo Levi, who was visiting Auschwitz when Israel invaded Lebanon, wrote that for him the 'two experiences were superimposed in an agonizing way'. The Italian writer had known the barbarities of the death camp at the same time as Améry; he translated the latter's work into Italian and kept by his side a copy of Améry's *On Suicide* (1976), a book that defined suicide as a 'summing up of many humiliations'. Like Améry, Levi had not grown up a Zionist, but he recognised that his relationship to Israel could not but be 'obvious and profound'. On his epic journey back to Italy from Auschwitz in 1945, Levi had come across young people from Eastern Europe. 'Extremely determined and confident,' he wrote, 'they were young Zionists, they were going to Israel, taking any route they could and by any means they could . . . They felt immensely free and strong, masters of the world and of their destiny.' Though Israeli readers had evinced little interest in his books for decades, Levi had continued to feel an emotional affinity to the Jewish state. He proudly told a bookseller in Turin how, with its blue and white colours, the cover of his novel *If Not Now, When?* cleverly wore the Israeli flag.

The novel was published in 1982, the same year as the Israeli destruction of Lebanon. Yet Levi drafted an open letter of protest, which, signed by Natalia Ginzburg, among other Italian writers, called for an immediate withdrawal of Israeli troops from Lebanon and an end to the construction of Jewish settlements in the occupied territories. Palestinian activists in Italy nevertheless accused him of being a mouthpiece for Zionism and conservative Jews attacked him for allegedly undermining Israel. Undeterred, Levi gave a series of interviews to Italian periodicals. In one of them he said that 'Israel is rapidly falling into total isolation . . . We must choke off the impulses towards emotional solidarity with Israel to reason coldly on the mistakes of Israel's current ruling class. Get rid of that ruling class.' Writing to a friend, he wondered 'if I belong to the Jewish people at all'.

He had already been incensed by Begin's exploitation of the history of genocidal antisemitism. And now, as he saw it, Israel's massacres in Lebanon had 'polluted' the image of Jews throughout the world and unleashed a new wave of lethal prejudice. In 1982, unidentified militants bombed a synagogue in Rome, killing a child. Roald Dahl, an antisemite, felt emboldened enough to write in the *Literary Review*, a mainstream British periodical, in 1983 that, after Lebanon, 'we all started hating the

Jews. Never before in the history of man has a race of people switched so rapidly from being much-pitied victims to barbarous murderers. Never before has a race of people generated so much sympathy around the world and then, in the space of a lifetime, succeeded in turning that sympathy into hatred and revulsion.' By 1984, three years before he committed suicide, Levi was arguing that 'the centre of gravity of the Jewish world must turn back, must move out of Israel and back into the diaspora'.

Today, misgivings of the kind expressed by Améry and Levi are likely to be condemned as grossly antisemitic in Israel and across the West. It's worth remembering that many such re-examinations of Zionism's fate began early in the existence of the State of Israel. Dorothy Thompson, the world's most famous female journalist and a Zionist in the 1930s and early 1940s, who was expelled by Hitler from Germany in 1934 for her anti-Nazi reporting, turned into a critic of Zionism after discovering on a 1945 trip to Mandatory Palestine that extreme elements of the movement were ascendant. Denounced as an antisemite, she became one of the first to identify as dangerous 'the continual beating of the drums of anti-anti-Semitism' and the equation of anti-Zionism with antisemitism. 'This really amounts to making anti-Semites, by appointment, of everybody who either does not believe in Zionism or criticizes any phase of Zionist and Israeli policy,' she wrote in *Commentary* in March 1950. She advised Jewish Americans, too, against an exacerbated consciousness of persecution. 'For when a fear takes possession of the mind, the pattern of behavior becomes self-defeating and of such a nature as to make the realization of the fear more likely . . . a primary neurosis is the fear of rejection and that when that neurosis takes hold of a person he unconsciously strives to create the conditions for that rejection.'

Deeper anxieties about the place and perception of Jews in the world were incited among survivors and witnesses of the Shoah after it became clear in 1967 that Israel had become a colonial power in the Middle East. The Egyptian writer Lotfallah Soliman predicted that same year that Palestinians, 'living under the conditions of a colonized people, are going to attain political consciousness and conduct a war of national liberation'. He saw that 'in reaping a lightning victory, Israel has done what the Germans did. Qua Israel, it has rushed into a grave.' The anguished Jewish observers of Israel may not have shared this prescient view of a Palestinian nationalist awakening; they could still see that Israel, ruling a conquered people while fanatical Zionists sought expansion into Greater Israel, had exposed itself to profound political and spiritual corruption. A year after the Six Day War, the Israeli historian Jacob Talmon wrote: 'I am not enough of a chauvinist to believe that the Jews are exempt from the snares and perversions which lie in wait for all mankind . . . For an Israel which lost its old bearings – Jewish, liberal, and idealistic – would become repulsively similar to the arch persecutors of the Jews.'

The following year Yeshayahu Leibowitz, a highly regarded philosopher who would win the Israel Prize in 1993, warned against the 'Nazification' of Israel. In 1981, the Israeli columnist Boaz Evron carefully described the stages of this moral corrosion: the tactic of conflating Palestinians with Nazis and shouting that another Shoah is imminent was, he feared, liberating ordinary Israelis from 'any moral restrictions, since one who is in danger of annihilation sees himself exempted from any moral considerations which might restrict his efforts to save himself'. Jews, Evron wrote, could end up treating 'non-Jews as subhuman' and replicating 'racist Nazi attitudes'.

Evron urged caution, too, against Israel's then new and ardent supporters. Much global bafflement was aroused by the recent spectacle of the comedian Jerry Seinfeld, who posed with a machine gun at an IDF training facility in the West Bank, taunted pro-Palestinian protesters, and claimed that he 'miss[es] a dominant masculinity'. However, already in the late 1970s, Israel was attracting this unusual kind of visitor and potential immigrant from the United States. Israel, a journalist in Philip Roth's novel *The Counterlife* (1986) says, 'was supposed to be the place where to become a normal Jew

was the goal'. But 'the ones who come from America are
either religious or crazy or both'.

> The American Jews get a big thrill from the guns. They
> see Jews walking around with guns and they think
> they're in paradise. Reasonable people with a civilized
> repugnance for violence and blood, they come on tour
> from America, and they see the guns and they see the
> beards, and they take leave of their senses. The beards
> to remind them of saintly Yiddish weakness and the
> guns to reassure them of heroic Hebrew force. Jews
> ignorant of history, Hebrew, Bible, ignorant of Islam
> and the Middle East, they see the guns and they see the
> beards, and out of them flows every sentimental emo-
> tion that wish fulfillment can produce.

For many in the Jewish American population, Evron
argued, championing Israel had become 'necessary
because of the loss of any other focal point to their
Jewish identity' – indeed, so great was their existential
lack that they did not wish Israel to become free of its
mounting dependence on Jewish American support.

> They need to feel needed. They also need the 'Israeli
> hero' as a social and emotional compensation in a
> society in which the Jew is not usually perceived as
> embodying the characteristics of the tough manly
> fighter. Thus, the Israeli provides the American Jew

with a double, contradictory image – the virile super-man, and the potential Holocaust victim – both of whose components are far from reality.

Zygmunt Bauman, the Polish-born Jewish philosopher and refugee from Nazism who spent three years in Israel after the Six Day War before fleeing its mood of bellicose righteousness, despaired of what he saw as the 'privati-sation' of the Shoah by Israel and its supporters. It has come to be remembered, he wrote in 1989, 'as a private experience of the Jews, as a matter between the Jews and their haters', even as the conditions that made acts of mass cruelty possible – bureaucratic specialisation, the attenuation of personal responsibility, the liberation of technology from ethical constraints accompanying an assault on minorities, and the destruction of intellec-tual pluralism – were appearing again around the world.

Such witnesses of Nazism, who had been plunged from a serene belief in secular humanism into collective insanity, intuited that the violence they had survived – unprecedented in its magnitude – wasn't an aberration in an essentially sound modern civilisation. Nor could it be blamed entirely on a hoary prejudice against Jews. Technology, the rational division of labour and defer-ence to norm-setting authority had enabled ordinary people to contribute to acts of mass extermination with a clear conscience, even with frissons of virtue. Prevent-ive efforts against such impersonal and available modes of killing required more than vigilance against antisemitism. And Nazi violence had to be seen as part of the destructive dynamic of modern political and economic systems – competitive racist colonialisms, environmental devastation, hunger and statelessness.

When I recently turned to my books to prepare a lecture, I found I'd already underlined many of passages I quote here. In my diary there are lines copied from the literary critic George Steiner ('the nation-state bristling with arms is a bitter relic, an absurdity in the century of crowded men') and the Israeli diplomat Abba Eban ('It is about time that we stand on our own feet and not on those of the six million dead'). Most of these annotations date back to the months after my first visit in 2008 to Israel and its occupied territories, when I was seeking to answer, in my innocence, two baffling questions: how did Israel, a country built to house a persecuted and homeless people, come to exercise such a terrible power of life and death over another population of refugees (many of them refugees in their own land); and how can the Western political and journalistic mainstream ignore, even justify, its clearly systematic cruelties and injustices?

I cannot answer these questions without invoking my own formation as a writer born and educated in India. Jacob Talmon once wrote, while warning Israel against international ostracism, that 'yesterday's victims of racist imperialism, the Third World, China, India ... were stone deaf to the magic sound of "Zion" and "Jerusalem", and unreceptive to any feelings of awe before the uniqueness of the Jewish fate'. This had never been true for me, an Indian whom modern history's tidy categories placed among yesterday's victims of racist imperialism. At different times in my life, and in diverse ways, I had been aware of the uniqueness of the Jewish fate, and felt an affinity to it.

Growing up in India in the 1970s, I had a picture on my wall of Moshe Dayan, Israel's defence minister during the Six Day War. This infatuation with Israeli heroes was irresistible partly because it was glamorously illicit in India. After the election of Narendra Modi in 2014, India and Israel seemed natural allies. In 2017 Modi and Netanyahu were pictured frolicking on a beach in Israel. India is now the Israeli defence industry's biggest foreign customer; Indian security forces deploy Israel's know-how in their occupation of Kashmir; Indian intelligence agencies use Israeli-made spyware to surveil politicians, rights activists and journalists; and Gautam Adani, the businessman closest to Modi, who operates Israel's biggest deep-water port in Haifa, and has a joint venture with Israel's largest arms producer Elbit Systems, sent made-in-India military drones to the country during its war on Gaza. But the intimacy belies a long and complex history defined by antagonism.

India's foremost anti-colonial leaders such as Gandhi

and Nehru repeatedly declared their sympathy for European Jews. Speaking to the *Jewish Chronicle* in London in 1931, Gandhi claimed to 'understand the longing of a Jew to return to Palestine', adding that 'he can do so if he can without the help of bayonets, whether his own or those of Britain' and 'in perfect friendliness with the Arabs'. Writing as early as July 1933, six months after the sudden apotheosis of Hitler in Germany, to his teenaged daughter Indira, later India's prime minister, Nehru denounced the 'mad racial obsession' of the Nazis. Responding to Kristallnacht in November 1938, Nehru proposed that his party, the Congress, offer employment in India to Jewish refugees.

As a member of the United Nations Special Committee on Palestine, India advocated together with Iran and Yugoslavia a plan, comprising autonomous Arab and Jewish states within a unified federal Palestine. The plan was defeated, and subsequently India joined Asian and African countries in voting against the United Nations resolution in November 1947 to divide Palestine into Jewish and Arab states. In a letter to Albert Einstein, who had pleaded with him to support the establishment of a Jewish state, Nehru wrote, 'I confess that while I have a very great deal of sympathy for the Jews I feel sympathy for the Arabs also . . . I know that the Jews have done a wonderful piece of work in Palestine and have raised the standards of the people there, but one question troubles me. After all these remarkable achievements, why have they failed to gain the goodwill of the Arabs?' In May 1949 India opposed Israel's admission to the United Nations and then withheld full diplomatic relations with the Jewish state until 1992.

Normal relations seemed briefly possible in the early 1950s. But Nehru, a personal friend of President Gamal Abdel Nasser of Egypt, was angered by Israeli collusion in the British and French attempt to seize the Suez Canal in 1956. Successive Indian governments dominated by Nehru's Congress Party championed the cause of Palestinians and routinely denounced Israel for its denial of rights to them. In 1974, India became one of the first non-Arab countries to recognise the Palestine Liberation Organisation as the 'sole and legitimate representative of the Palestinian people'. India was also one of the first non-Arab countries to recognise the State of Palestine when the PLO proclaimed it in 1988. In November 1975, India joined Islamic countries in voting for UN General Assembly Resolution 3379 that denounced Zionism as 'a form of racism and racial discrimination'.

But many Indians, especially upper-caste Hindu nationalists, were proud and eager to break the official consensus against Israel defined by Nehru and his successors in the Congress Party. This was largely because of the emotional and ideological affinity Hindu nationalists felt with Zionists. Both Jewish and Hindu nationalisms had emerged in the late nineteenth century out of an experience of marginality and humiliation.

Many of their radical ideologists longed to overcome what they perceived as a shameful lack of manhood among Jews and Hindus. Most Hindu nationalists shared the hard-nosed realism of Jabotinsky who in an early essay pointed out that man is a wolf to man. 'We will not change this through political reforms, nor through culture and even bitter experience will not change it,' he wrote. 'Justice exists only for those whose fists and stubbornness make it possible for them to realize it.'

This was also the nation-building logic of Vinayak Damodar Savarkar, Jabotinsky's Hindu counterpart, one of whose followers assassinated Gandhi in January 1948 for failing to be wolf-like to Muslims. In the immediate countrywide crackdown ordered by Nehru on Hindu nationalists, my relatives were among those arrested or forced to go underground. One of them, my grandfather, introduced me to Moshe Dayan's legend. He recounted keenly how the IDF general had outmanoeuvred numerically superior Arab armies in 1967; how he had snatched the Golan Heights from Syria at the last minute. When news leaked of Dayan's secret visit in 1977 as Israel's foreign minister to India's first non-Congress government, and pictures of him appeared in the Indian newspapers, I was transfixed by his black eye-patch and mischievous grin. This image of Israeli vitality, courage and resourcefulness was confirmed by one of the first books that I read in English: William Stevenson's *Ninety Minutes at Entebbe* (1976), an account of the audacious rescue from Entebbe Airport in Uganda of 103 Israeli hostages from the Air France flight hijacked by German and Palestinian militants (Netanyahu, whose older brother was killed in the operation, traces the start of his political journey to this event).

Bookstalls in even remote Indian railway stations always displayed paperback copies of Leon Uris's novel *Exodus* (1958), another romantic narrative about the creation of Israel. David Ben-Gurion reportedly said of the novel that 'as a literary work, it isn't much. But as a piece of propaganda, it's the greatest thing ever written about Israel.' Certainly, the fictionalised drama of the SS *Exodus 1947*, the ship that sailed to Palestine from Europe carrying over 4,500 refugees in an attempt to break the British blockade of Palestine, was a stirring lesson in the need for both resolute self-defence and perpetual suspicion of perfidious Muslims. Other cheap paperbacks I read at this time, such as Frederick Forsyth's *The Odessa File* (1972), in which vengeful Nazis collaborate with Arabs to destroy Israel, reinforced my identification with Zionism. And for Hindu nationalists in the 1970s, reduced then to being impotent detractors of the ruling pro-Palestinian Congress Party, Jabotinsky's heirs such as Begin, Ariel Sharon and Yitzhak Shamir seemed to have won the race to muscular nationhood. The envy is now out of the closet: far-right Hindu trolls constitute Benjamin Netanyahu's largest fan club in the world.

Zionism really was to us a wistful historical romance,

in which a prodigious quest, full of tragedies and set-backs, culminates in a near-miraculous event: the founding of Israel. In comparison, Hindu nationalism seemed like a tragedy: deprived of a united country by Muslim separatists, softheaded Gandhi (and Nehru) allowed a catastrophic partition of British-ruled India in 1947 that led to the slaughter and rape of count-less Hindus. Worse: the newly created state of Pakistan occupied a part of Muslim-majority Kashmir; mean-while, tens of millions of Muslims remained in India, an apparently formidable fifth column for Pakistan. Hindu nationalists were also marginalised humiliatingly by the political and cultural dominance of an avowedly secular political party, the Congress.

We came to admire Israel because it seemed to pos-sess a proud and clear self-image, and a religious and cultural ideology that commanded spontaneous loyalty from its citizens. Nation-building in seemingly splendid isolation, Israel was also an example of how to deal with Muslims in the only language they understood: that of force and more force. India, in comparison, seemed a pitiably incoherent and timid nation state, its claims to democracy, socialism and secularism compromised by a corrupt government's appeasement of Muslims and neglect of Hindu heritage.

Of Western antisemitism, whether the blaming of Jews for Christ's murder or conspiracy-mongering about

Jewish world domination through capitalism or communism, we knew nothing. India was one of the Asian and African countries where Jews had lived relatively unmolested for centuries. The Sassoons of Bombay supported gruesome British reprisals against Indian mutineers in 1857; they were also complicit in the opium trade between India and China. Yet, as Jonathan Kaufman relates in *The Last Kings of Shanghai* (2020), the Sassoons and Kadoories, another Jewish business family from Baghdad, were identified in resentful Asian eyes as British imperialists and compradors rather than as Jews, and the antisemitic bigotry they suffered came from other British businessmen in Asia.

As early as May 1933, a delegation including such luminaries of Chinese politics and culture as Madame Sun Yat-sen, Cai Yuanpei, Lu Xun and Lin Yutang lodged a strong protest with the German consul in Shanghai against Nazi treatment of Jews. Ho Feng-Shan, the Chinese consul in Vienna in 1938, encouraged Jews waiting futilely at Western diplomatic missions to apply for an exit visa from him. Unlike other destinations, Shanghai didn't require a separate entry document, and between 1933 and 1941, Shanghai gave asylum to 18,000 Jews from Europe: a figure that exceeds the number of Jewish refugees taken by Canada, New Zealand, South Africa and British India *combined* during the Second World War.

Subsequent readings in the scholarship of Western Judaeophobia have not remedied my basic bafflement over its intensity and scale, or that the Germans were joined by the French, Italians, Austrians, Poles, Ukrainians, Lithuanians, Latvians, Croatians in envying and despising Jews and then in trying to cleanse the world of them.* Even the Japanese militarists who had embraced the fabrications of *The Protocols of the Elders of Zion* were appalled when the German SS arrived in Japan-occupied Shanghai with a plan to exterminate the city's Jewish refugees. The American soldiers who liberated the Jewish ghetto in Shanghai in September 1945 braced themselves for the abominations seen by their compatriots in Nazi-occupied Europe. They found what the historian David Kranzler later called the 'Miracle of Shanghai': though the ghetto's inhabitants had suffered from poverty and malnutrition, just about all of them had survived.

Of the Shoah, too, we knew almost next to nothing. Awareness of it was not much advanced even in the West until the 1970s. In India, as well as in other parts of the decolonised world, public remembrance was focused on the local atrocities of white supremacism, such as the British massacre of hundreds of unarmed Indians in Amritsar in 1919, or the genocidal Bengal Famine of 1943 exacerbated by Winston Churchill's hatred of Hindus. An illustrated book on war in my father's small

---

* Muslim-majority Albania was an exception: sheltering refugees, it emerged from the war with a much greater Jewish population than it had in 1939.

library included the well-known picture of a boy holding his hands above his head as an SS officer points a sub-machine gun at him during the Warsaw Ghetto uprising of 1943. I remember being struck by this image of extreme vulnerability, as much as I was by the photograph of the little Vietnamese girl running naked down a dusty road, away from her village, aflame with American napalm. But I had no means to isolate it from the broad panorama of war and suffering.

This obliviousness to European and Jewish history made it possible for Hindu nationalists to enviously admire Nazism as well as Zionism. M. S. Golwalkar, the much-revered Hindu leader and ideologue, had written in 1939 how Nazi Germany was manifesting 'race pride at its highest' by purging itself of the 'Semitic Races'. *Mein Kampf* has remained a perennial bestseller in India, selectively read and celebrated for its lessons in nation-building rather than its loathing of Jews (and Indians). Like many Hindu nationalists, present as well as past, my grandfather could comfortably balance his approval of Hitler's patriotism with his support for Zionism. After all, both Nazi Germany and Israel seemed determined to cleanse their states of alien and potentially disloyal elements, and encourage a militaristic ethos among their citizens.

Such ideological and emotional overlaps are common in history. Jabotinsky himself believed in racial pride and racial superiority, and fulsomely endorsed Ukrainian nationalism in the early twentieth century even as it became identified with anti-Jewish pogroms. As I grew older, and my childish infatuation with crude strength faded, I began to be aware of another kind of congruence with modern Jewish experience.

Jews were not Asian like the Parsis, I realised, despite the seemingly Oriental cast of many synagogues, and the importance of Jewish entrepreneurs in the globalising business communities of pre-war India and China. Yet their place in the occident was not unlike those of the Oriental children of colonial modernity – the peoples of Asian and African ancestry who came belatedly to Western civilisation, and were consequently forced to confront the challenge of living with plural identities and cultural loyalties. The famous mid-eighteenth-century journey of Moses Mendelssohn, a promising young religious scholar, from a medieval ghetto to Berlin, and the transformation through a thicket of prejudice of a young provincial into a renowned German writer, seemed to have its closest parallels in the Asian and African journeys from the periphery to the metropolis.

Modern Europeans deemed these peoples of the periphery to be too weak and backward to be consequential in world history. Hegel had sneered at Jews as much as he did at Asians and Africans while elaborating his philosophy of universal development. Yet all these subjects of his condescension had emerged out of the restrictions and obligations of traditional society and grasped at the promises held out by modern ideologies of emancipation; they had struggled simultaneously to achieve dignity and fresh identity in a milieu not their own.

In the nineteenth and early twentieth centuries, many Asians, Africans and Jews fervently endorsed the idea of assimilation to the dominant society and culture. Acting on the belief that their future lay in apprenticing themselves to modern Europe, upper-caste Hindus in the eastern Indian state of Bengal initiated what is called the Bengal, and often the Indian, Renaissance. Many young Jews in the Pale of Settlement became keen disciples of Russia's high culture, memorising Pushkin's verses in a bid to escape what Osip Mandelstam called 'the Judaic chaos'. German-speaking Jews simultaneously found irresistible the German bourgeois ideal of *Bildung*, which combined conventional education with the personal cultivation of reason and aesthetic taste, and proposed to exalt individuals sunk in mindless superstition to enlightenment.

Such assimilation required the easing of old taboos, especially on food, and the embrace of new languages, names, clothes and even religion – conversion to Christianity was the most dramatic (and commonplace) of makeovers among Asians, Africans and European Jews alike.* At the same time, totems of successful assimilation,

---

* Baptism, the poet Heinrich Heine, a Jewish convert to Lutheranism, famously said, was 'the price of admission to European culture'.

such as Gerson Bleichröder, private banker to Bismarck, and Walther Rathenau, foreign minister in Weimar Germany, remained relatively rare; and in any case the outward success hid much private torment. More common was the experience of futile striving, poisoned by fear, obsequious sycophancy, self-denial and self-reproach.

Gandhi, an Anglophile for the first decades of his life, remembers in his autobiography the pitiable time when he 'vied with Englishmen in loyalty to the throne'.* During his three-year sojourn in London, Gandhi tried his hand at 'playing the English Gentleman' by taking elocution, French and dancing lessons, and wearing 'a chimney-pot hat costing nineteen shillings' and 'an evening suit made in Bond Street'; he 'wasted ten minutes every day before a huge mirror, watching myself arranging my tie and parting my hair in the correct fashion', all in order to 'look the thing'.

---

* It was as a hyper-patriotic subject of Queen Victoria that the foremost anti-imperialist began his struggle for equality. It is instructive to compare Gandhi's trajectory to that of the Tory politician Benjamin Disraeli, who was born to a Jewish family but baptised at age twelve. Disraeli never ceased to be more royalist than the queen, and gave, while climbing social ladders in Britain, intellectual respectability to nineteenth-century racism. His most recent biographer David Cesarani claims that 'Disraeli almost single-handedly invented the lexicon of modern racial anti-Semitism'. One of his admirers was Adolf Hitler, who in a 1941 speech said, 'The British Jew, Lord Disraeli, once said that the racial problem was the key to world history. We National Socialists have grown up with that idea.'

Yet racial degradations – crucially, his expulsion from a whites-only train compartment in South Africa – reminded Gandhi that he would never be permitted into the ranks of English gentlemen or treated with parity in a society to which he did not belong from birth. The painful experience – the self-contempt of the parvenu, followed by social humiliation – launched his eccentric quest for a homeland where values other than worldly success were honoured. The same social and political insecurity seemed to confront many Jews despite their having achieved economic well-being and intellectual confidence.

'The only race greater than the Jews,' the Harrow-educated scion of the Sassoons, Victor, reportedly wisecracked, 'is the Derby' – the horse race favoured by British aristocrats in which he entered his own thoroughbreds. For much of his life, Sir Victor Sassoon radiated the pride of belonging to the 'international society of the successful' – the only one, as Arendt pointed out, 'in which Jews enjoyed equal rights'. Yet, languishing expensively in the Bahamas after the Communist revolution in China, this former 'king of Shanghai' complained bitterly of the parties he had not been invited to. Rathenau in Germany similarly worked hard to stress his fastidious distance, as acculturated Jew, from the public behaviour of his fellow Jews, the 'Asiatic horde', as he called them. But neither his success as a businessman nor his patriotism and intellectual dandyism shielded him from murderous prejudice – he was assassinated in 1922.

Indeed, the more I read of Jewish history the more compellingly familiar I found the cruel Jewish experience of modernity. More than the peoples from Asia and Africa, Jews had been defined as alien to the West, the undesirable embodiment of the non-West within the West – the 'Asiatic horde'. Marx, regarding himself as a cosmopolitan citizen of the world, privately denounced his foppish friend Ferdinand Lassalle as a 'Jewish nigger'. But both remained Jews in Gentile eyes however fervently and ostentatiously they renounced their Jewish ancestry, or imagined a new social order in which it would become irrelevant.

In his top hat, coat-tails and white gloves, Theodor Herzl, the founder of political Zionism, was the very epitome of a late-nineteenth-century Western bourgeois liberal – the beneficiary of the full civil equality decreed for Jews in Germany and Austria–Hungary in the 1860s and 70s. Yet by the 1890s, he was forced to acknowledge that the assurance of freedom and equality held out by assimilation was treacherous. The post-Enlightenment commitment to a new social contract – the promise of political community in which religious belief or ethnic origin of citizens would have no bearing on their rights – had proved deceptive.

The tone of betrayal is unmistakable in the famous dedication of Nirad Chaudhuri's *The Autobiography of an*

Unknown Indian (1951), a devoted Anglophile's lament over the abysmal failure of the Indian Renaissance, which he blamed on British racism: 'To the memory of the British Empire in India, which conferred subjecthood on us but withheld citizenship.' The sense of futility was stronger among those European Jews who championed *Bildung* after forsaking all that appeared to be a barrier to their social acceptance, and then found themselves victimised in Europe's nineteenth-century maelstrom.

The secular individualistic modernity they longed for in the ghetto and the shtetl turned out to be inseparable from a new tribal religion across Europe: nationalism, many versions of it, each jealously exclusive with its own golden age of ethnic-racial harmony, and sharp sense of those who did not belong – the 'other'. Far from being banished, racism had become an ineradicable feature of the modern West, supported by pseudo-science, and demagogues had found in antisemitism an easy and cheap distraction from the fundamentally irresolvable social and economic problems of industrial capitalism, a system prone to periodic malfunction that, while promising wealth and social mobility to the uprooted, generated extreme inequality and profound feelings of humiliation and resentment.

Jewish contributions had proved to be crucial in the making of this new and much-despised economic order in the nineteenth century, and its emergence as an intricately interdependent global entity. From London to Shanghai, Jews constituted a high proportion among those who connected different and distant parts of the world with financial and commercial innovations and entrepreneurship, and created secular public cultures by founding news agencies, periodicals and publishing houses.* So spectacular was the success of a restlessly innovative Jewish minority – a minority completely unrepresentative of Jews in general – that it would become the very symbol of the modern world made by capitalism, inviting the hostility of those expelled from, or nostalgic for, the pre-modern past. 'From early on,' Kafka wrote worriedly to Max Brod in 1920, '[Jews] have forced upon Germany things that she might have arrived at slowly and in her own way, but which she was opposed to because they stemmed from strangers.'

As ancient Jew-hatred mutated into racial antisemitism (the word itself was coined in the 1870s), integration assumed a derogatory connotation, implying mindless imitation and loss of authentic self. Struggling with their

---

* Yuri Slezkine writes in *The Jewish Century* (2004) that 'in early twentieth-century Germany, Austria, and Hungary, most of the national newspapers that were not specifically Christian or anti-Semitic were owned, managed, edited, and staffed by Jews'. In *The Years of Persecution, 1933–1939* (1997), Saul Friedländer details 'a strong Jewish presence in ownership, editorial responsibility, and major cultural or political commentary'.

anguished predicament – of people escaping from their own traditional culture but not admitted to any of the other established modern cultures of nationalism – many Jews turned to defining an international vision of salvation. Certainly, no Gentiles could compare in their passion for global human equality with Karl Marx, Rosa Luxemburg and Leon Trotsky. Jews across the West were prominent among those who upheld the equal and inalienable rights of man, and ideas of universal natural law and popular sovereignty. But this identification with liberal cosmopolitanism and socialist universalism only helped further identify Jews in many envious or merely confused eyes with all the hated shocks and disruptions of modernity.

By the early twentieth century, antisemitic violence and lack of economic opportunity forced millions of European and Russian Jews to immigrate to the United States. Among some of those who stayed the idea of a Jewish homeland emerged as another likely solution to the problems caused by political and economic modernisation. It seemed that the torments of the spiritually uprooted man, who according to early Zionist Max Nordau 'has lost his home in the ghetto, and he is denied a home in his native land', could only be healed among his own kind.

For decades, however, Europe's social outcasts and unwitting victims of modernity abjured the political remedy of Zionism, sensing in it a dark mimicry of the nationalisms that persecuted them. Rather, whether as leftists or Jewish nationalists, they evolved, as Arendt wrote, 'out of their personal experience Jewish poets, writers, and artists', the 'concept of the pariah as a human type – a concept of supreme importance for the evaluation of mankind in our day'. Their status as outsiders, lacking the prestige of ancestry and the establishment, made them upstarts and usurpers in Western society, a marginality underlined by eruptions of racial prejudice.

Travelling through Iran and Turkey in the early twentieth century, a time of vicious pogroms, the Russian writer Viktor Shklovsky felt the 'East' to be more congenial because 'there was no antisemitism' there. Living in the so-called East, I felt a great affinity to the distinctive early-twentieth-century Jewish experience of estrangement: the experience of a 'transitional' people, as Kafka described them in his stirring letter to his father, which had migrated from the 'still comparatively devout countryside to the cities'. It confirmed that a socially mobile people, denied both a secure habitat in the modern world and unconscious intimacy with a collective past, were doomed to know more than their human share of shame and guilt.

Certainly, those who grew up in India calling their mothers 'Mummy' in the coloniser's language could instinctively grasp Kafka's anguished realisation that 'I did not always love my mother as she deserved and as

I could, only because the German language prevented it. The Jewish mother is no *Mutter*, to call her *Mutter* makes her a little comic.' When Osip Mandelstam wrote of recoiling in horror from 'the Judaic chaos' of his Yiddish-speaking grandparents' home, and the 'vulgar' speech of the rabbi at his childhood synagogue, the anglophone, socially mobile Indian reader remorsefully recognised a similar source of revulsion in his own life.

A commonplace insight defines Jews as the critical conscience of the modern world, and credits Marx, Freud, Einstein and Lévi-Strauss as having both defined and problematised our very sense of reality. But there is more to be said, I always felt, about how the sense of inner duality known by other unaccommodated peoples of modernity was also felt by Jews in the late nineteenth and early twentieth centuries. W. E. B. Du Bois, who was routinely mistaken for a Jew in Germany and Eastern Europe,* defined a 'double-consciousness' in his 1903 classic *The Souls of Black Folk*: 'this sense of always looking at one's self through the eyes of others, of measuring one's soul by the tape of a world that looks on in amused contempt and pity'. In 1956, Richard Wright described this ambiguous existence defined by perpetual inner

---

* His professor in Berlin was Heinrich von Treitschke, who notoriously proclaimed that 'the Jews are our misfortune'; Du Bois also heard him say, 'mulattoes are inferior! They feel themselves inferior.'

anxiety and social awkwardness from the perspective of a non-Jewish 'nigger': 'Being a Negro living in a white Western Christian society, I've never been allowed to blend, in a natural and healthy manner, with the culture and civilization of the West. This contradiction of being both Western and a man of color creates a psychological distance, so to speak, between me and my environment. I'm self-conscious. I admit it.'

And in one writer after another – Kafka, Proust, Joseph Roth, Isaac Babel, Boris Pasternak, Osip Mandelstam – I discovered this self-consciousness born out of a restless solitude, and a need to adjust oneself to others, heightened into psychological acumen, ironic wit, scepticism, iconoclastic insight and artistic achievement. I grew attached to this sensibility, nurtured deep within the ruins of a much longed-for but compromised and tragically unachievable modernity. This complicated structure of feeling – akin to what the Jewish Russian writer Svetlana Boym called the 'off-modern' – seemed so strikingly and unusually congenial among an ostensibly Western and white people, and represented in a staggering array of artists, writers, scholars and political activists.

I delighted in the entangled modernity of Jews and Orientals I came across in my own work: the fruitful encounters between Ignaz Goldziher, the pioneering Jewish Hungarian scholar of Islam, and the Muslim world's most influential thinker and activist in the nineteenth century, Jamal ad-Din Al-Afghani.* I remember discovering, at a Muslim graveyard in Delhi, the tomb of Gerda Philipsborn, the much-revered German Jewish educationist who fled Germany in 1932 (leaving behind her lover, the nuclear physicist Leo Szilard) and found refuge among India's anti-colonialist intellectuals and activists.

Days before being deported to Treblinka in 1942, Janusz Korczak, a renowned Polish author of children's literature and child psychologist by profession, had staged one of Tagore's most famous plays, *Dak Ghar* ('The Post Office') with the children at his orphanage in the Warsaw Ghetto. The play's protagonist is an orphaned boy, who develops a rich imaginative life while dying of a terminal illness. Was this Korczak's way of preparing the orphans of the Warsaw Ghetto for the death camp? He himself had refused all offers to leave the ghetto and save his life. In the film *Korczak* (1990) by the great Polish director Andrzej Wajda, Korczak marches together with his children, singing cheerfully, to the site of deportation. I was intrigued, too, to find out that Korczak, a deeply devout man fascinated by

---

* Major nineteenth-century Jewish scholars and writers such as Goldziher, Abraham Geiger, Heinrich Graetz and Gustav Weil helped de-orientalise Islam in Western eyes, presenting it as rational and tolerant, akin to reform Judaism. They also repeatedly contrasted Muslim accommodation of Jews to their maltreatment by Christians.

Asian religions, had dreamed while living in the ghetto of Tagore (or Rabbi Tagore, as Einstein playfully called his friend).

I started to see, too, the ways in which the prejudices of white supremacists across the West connected Jewish to Asian and African fates. In *Black Skin, White Masks* (1952), Frantz Fanon recounts his philosophy teacher in the Antilles telling him, 'When you hear someone insulting the Jews, pay attention; he is talking about you.'* It was clearer, perhaps, in the colonial peripheries than in the West that throughout their escalating military conflicts and economic rivalries, all Western powers, democratic or authoritarian, collaborated in upholding a racial hierarchy – the project of keeping, as the first liberal internationalist US president, Woodrow Wilson, baldly stated in 1917, 'the white race strong' and preserving 'white civilisation and its domination of the planet'.

The Shoah itself seemed to have been partly enabled by decades of unprecedented violence and a rhetoric of racial and civilisational superiority that bolstered national and individual self-esteem, pre-emptively defusing the likelihood of guilt. General Arthur MacArthur (father of Douglas) amplified then commonplace ideas

---

* In *Lines of Descent* (2014), Kwame Anthony Appiah excavates an undated jotting from the Du Bois archives: 'Suddenly came the thought – are Jews black? do they know, have they suffered?'

in the West when, in a Senate hearing on the killings of more than 200,000 civilians during the US conquest of the Philippines between 1898 and 1902, he referred to the 'magnificent Aryan peoples' he belonged to and the 'unity of the race' he felt compelled to uphold. So did the German Kaiser when in 1900 he dispatched German troops on a joint Western mission of racial vengeance against rebellious Chinese, urging them to 'give no pardon and take no prisoners', and to make sure that 'no Chinese will ever even dare to look askance at a German'.

In *Mein Kampf* Hitler described African soldiers serving in the French army during the French occupation of the Rhineland between 1918 and 1930 as a Jewish conspiracy aimed at 'bastardising' white people and turning Jews into their masters. The founder of Nazism, who admired the US's unequivocally racist policies of citizenship, anti-miscegenation and immigration, and revered such American flagbearers of antisemitism as Henry Ford and Madison Grant, was expressing ideas then travelling back and forth across the Atlantic. The Nazis who in 1937 forcibly sterilised hundreds of children fathered by African soldiers took direct inspiration from American innovations in racial hygiene. In *War Against the Weak* (2003), Edwin Black shows that 'the idea of sending the unfit into lethal chambers was regularly bandied about in the United States', decades before

Nevada approved one such chamber for criminal executions in 1921.*

In the late 1930s, as eugenicists across America delightedly sought vindication in Hitler's systematic elimination of the unfit, including Jews, from German society, Churchill eloquently refused to admit 'that a great wrong has been done to the Red Indians of America or the black people of Australia' since 'a stronger race, a higher-grade race, a more worldly wise race to put it that way, has come in and taken their place'. Churchill's wartime policies that helped kill millions of Hindus (a 'beastly people with a beastly religion', according to him) enraged one of his own Cabinet colleagues into comparing the British prime minister to the German Führer. At exactly the same time, Hitler was airing his obsessions with what he saw as the efficient British exploitation of India and the American genocidal conquest of Native American lands.†

During the Nazi war of annihilation in the Soviet Union, he spoke often of Ukraine as 'that new Indian Empire' and the Volga as 'our Mississippi'. In his

---

* Even the Nazis found eugenic policies in the United States too radical for their taste, as Stefan Kühl relates in *The Nazi Connection* (1994).

† One of Hitler's favourite films was *The Lives of a Bengal Lancer* (1935), starring Gary Cooper, which visualised, more clearly than other propaganda products of the British Empire, his fantasy of strapping Aryans lording it over the lesser breeds.

imagination, pioneer farmer-soldier families would populate Poland, Belarus and Ukraine after the people present there, including Europe's largest population of Jews, had been killed, and an Aryan ruling class would burnish its martial virtues while serenely governing the conquered lands just as the British seemed to in India. The many examples of genocides ignored in history, or justified Churchill-style as essential steps in national and racial progress, encouraged Hitler to think that he would get away with his own final solution. In fact, Hitler shared his view of the 'Red Indians of America' with Churchill: 'we eat Canadian wheat and never think of the Indians'. 'Who, after all,' he also asked, 'is today speaking about the destruction of the Armenians?'*

Many subordinate peoples in Asia and Africa saw, well before Arendt wrote about them in *The Origins of Totalitarianism* (1951), the links between Western imperialism in Asia and Africa and Nazi imperialism in Europe. They had too forcefully been made aware of how ethnic-racial supremacy was the assurance of identity and dignity to many in the West; and they became naturally alert to the necessity for a Jewish homeland. Tagore repeatedly expressed support for it in his meetings with

* This was at least partly because in 1915 the German political class and media suppressed the facts of the genocide inflicted by their Ottoman allies on Armenians.

Martin Buber and Einstein in the 1920s and 30s. Writing to the founder of the Shanghai Zionist association, the father of Chinese nationalism Sun Yat-sen hailed Zionism in 1920 as 'one of the greatest movements of the present time'. In his famous lectures on nationalism in 1924, Sun upheld the 'national spirit' of Jews as a model for the Chinese.

However, as Indian voters succumbed to Hindu supremacists, I found myself turning to Indian critics of the nation state, such as Tagore, who denounced nationalist Asians as 'callow schoolboys of the East': they, he argued, had fallen for a Western idea with 'high-sounding distinction' but which was actually 'one of the most powerful anaesthetics that man has invented', under whose influence people can carry out a 'systematic programme of the most virulent self-seeking without being in the least aware of its moral perversion, – in fact feeling dangerously resentful if it is pointed out'.

I found Tagore's critique – that 'the people accept this all-pervading mental slavery with cheerfulness and pride because of their nervous desire to turn themselves into a machine of power, called the Nation, and emulate other machines in their collective worldliness' – echoed in the writings of Ahad Ha'am, the pioneering Hebrew writer and opponent of Herzl who likewise deplored the nationalist 'tendency to find the path of glory in the attainment of material power and political dominion'.

Both political Zionists and anti-colonialist nationalisms

internalised the damning accusations of their European detractors – that they were weak, cowardly and inferior, unfit for the task of nation-building – while longing to be transformed into strong, brave and superior men, magnificently equipped to establish a modern nation. Having embraced Tagore's strictures against Indian nationalism, I was fascinated to discover the often very strident denunciations of Zionism among Jews in the German-speaking countries, from Freud to Hannah Arendt.

Among a people in whom Mendelssohn had helped seed nearly two centuries of an unparalleled creative flowering, and the desire for a tolerant multicultural society, Zionism was largely anathema – until it was calamitously too late. Stefan Zweig was an early opponent of the Zionism his fellow journalist Herzl envisioned and did not change his mind. 'I see it as the mission of the Jews in the political sphere to uproot nationalism in every country,' he wrote in 1919. 'Having sown our blood and our ideas throughout the world for 2,000 years, we cannot go back to being a little nation in a corner of the Arab region.' Even while living in Dresden under Nazi rule in 1934, Victor Klemperer could write in his diary, 'To me the Zionists, who want to go back to the Jewish state of A.D. 70 (destruction of Jerusalem by Titus), are just as offensive as the Nazis. With their nosing after blood, their ancient "cultural roots", their partly canting, partly obtuse winding back of the world they are altogether a match for the National Socialists.' As late as 1939, Klemperer was still telling himself, 'The Jewish communities in Germany today are all extremely inclined to Zionism; I shall go along with that just as little as I do with National Socialism or with Bolshevism. Liberal and German *forever.*'

In retrospect, these Jewish expressions of faith in European liberalism make for tragic readings: Zweig, for instance, still claiming in *The World of Yesterday*, the memoir he wrote shortly before he committed suicide in desolate exile in Brazil, that Karl Lueger, the mayor of Vienna, and Hitler's role model, 'always maintained a certain chivalry towards his opponents, and his official antisemitism never stopped him from being helpful and friendly to his former Jewish friends'. I remember being moved to tears by *The Pity of It All* (2002), Amos Elon's account of the extraordinary Jewish infatuation with German culture, which ends with the advent of Hitler in early 1933 and premonitions of doom. The book's last words describe Hannah Arendt fleeing Berlin in the summer of that year on a train 'south through the rolling countryside, in the opposite direction taken two centuries earlier by the boy Moses Mendelssohn, on foot, on his way to fame and fortune in Enlightenment Berlin'.

When I finally began to learn systematically about the calamity visited upon Jews, Germany's assault on its assimilated, patriotic and *minuscule* (less than 1 per cent) minority seemed abominable enough. It struck me as unutterably vile that most countries in the West should become directly or indirectly complicit in the massacre of a people that had done more than any other to define what equal and cosmopolitan citizenship mean in the modern world. That the so-called Western democracies would refuse to lower their barriers of immigration to Jews escaping Nazism, leaving tens of thousands of them to find a safe haven in China. That one country after another in Europe would deliver its Jewish population to the Nazi death camps. That in Poland, Ukraine and the Baltic States eager local collaborators would hunt down Jews cowering in basements, attics and woods. That Walter Benjamin, one of the most incandescent writers of the twentieth century, should commit suicide out of the fear of being handed over to the Nazis in France by Spanish border guards.

I read about the Shoah, and watched the films and documentaries, out of a sense of obligation: to confront, or at least not turn away, from such an extreme example of human suffering, and to try to make some sense out of it. No clear understanding of course rewarded my reading and watching.

Some of what I read and watched made me more rather than less disorientated. I remember being very surprised by *Europa Europa* (1990), the film by Agnieszka Holland based on the real-life account of

Solomon 'Solly' Perel, a German Jew who survived the murder of his family only by suppressing his Jewishness and posing as an Aryan, in which capacity he dated a viciously antisemitic young woman and became a star member of the Hitler Youth. Rewarded with the most elementary form of success – he's alive at the end of the war – he moved to Israel and resolved proudly to live as a Jew.* The much-acclaimed film *Schindler's List* (1993), which gave to me and millions of other people their clearest images of the Shoah,[†] also upholds survival, or the ability to live while others die, as the supreme human value. When Ben Kingsley, playing a Jew in Steven Spielberg's film (but confusingly fixed in my mind as Gandhi from Richard Attenborough's biopic), is pulled out at the very last minute from a train destined for the death camps by his employer Schindler, the German businessman, I gasped in relief, like

---

* In an interview conducted in 2019 that accompanies the Criterion Collection edition of Holland's 1990 film, Perel upholds the idea of self-preservation for the sake of self-preservation, while reminiscing about his 'buddies' in the Hitler Youth and his former German girlfriend who wanted to conceive an Aryan child for her Führer.

† Albeit images corrupted by fantasy, such as the scene in which naked women crammed into a gas chamber look at showerheads, uncertain whether water or gas will emerge from them, and erupt in shrieks of relief on being anointed as survivors. Lawrence L. Langer, the most acute critic of the artistic exploitation of the Shoah, writes that 'more mischief has been spread about the killing process in Auschwitz by that single cinematic episode than any other media version of the Holocaust'.

probably millions of other viewers. It was only afterwards that I thought about the thousands of Jews who
remained on that train to Treblinka.

There was no emotional release of an even horribly
tainted kind in the story of the survivors of Treblinka
recounted in Gitta Sereny's *Into That Darkness* (1974).
The Nazis allowed a few conscripted labourers to live
as long as they helped expedite the extermination of the
thousands of Jews arriving on trains from different parts
of Europe. When arrivals slowed at the beginning of
1943, they were anxious and hungry for days. In March,
they grew excited when told that transports would be
resumed soon, and then pounced on the first train that
arrived: 24,000 rich Jews from Salonica, who were parted
from their sumptuous foods and belongings, and killed
in three days.*

* Sereny's book quotes at length one of the survivors who were ready,
even eager, to kill so that they could survive: 'It was just about when we
had reached the lowest ebb in our morale that, one day towards the end
of March, Kurt Franz walked into our barracks, a wide grin on his face.
"As of tomorrow," he said, "transports will be rolling in again." And do
you know what we felt? We said to ourselves, "Hurrah, at last we can
fill our bellies again." That's the truth; that's what we felt; that is where
we had got to. And sure enough, the next morning they arrived. We
had spent all of the preceding evening in an excited, expectant mood; it
meant life – you see, don't you? – safety and life. The fact that it was their
death, whoever they were, which meant our life, was no longer relevant;
we had been through this over and over and over. The main question
in our minds was, where were they from? Would they be rich or poor?
Would there be food or not?'

I was doing my reading during the years the savagery of genocide unfolded in Rwanda, Burundi and the former Yugoslavia, with victims equally innocent. And the genocidal imperialisms of the past driven by racist prejudice never ceased to resonate. In Auschwitz itself, the word *Muselmänner*, 'Muslims', was used, Primo Levi wrote, to describe men denuded of all will and dignity, and ripe for the gas chambers.*

Still, the single-mindedness of the Shoah's executioners, the premeditation and cold-bloodedness of those who envisioned, organised and constructed the factories for mass, swift and secretive death, or drew up inventories of all its lucrative by-products, appeared unthinkable. So did the bewilderment and terror of their victims. The experience of being reduced in the ghettos to eating dogs, cats and horses, of travelling days and nights in sealed boxcars, thirsty and starving, in proximity to corpses, of arriving, confused, at the camps, and then being driven to the gas chambers, the realisation dawning, as the door is sealed behind, that everyone is about to be killed – the fate of the doomed still seemed incredible in the way the death camps might have been to the people in the US and UK who first heard about

---

* Glossing these reflections by Levi, the Italian philosopher Giorgio Agamben writes that 'the Jews knew that they would not die at Auschwitz as Jews'. Rather, their fate had become indistinguishable from that of many other victims, all of whom, whether Jews or not, could be reduced in principle to the figure of the *Muselmänner*.

them and did nothing, except that the facts were all now incontrovertible. The monotony of cruelty killed curiosity, by making it seem a gruesome variant of voyeurism. And I knew anger and shame when I thought about the many Indians who read *Mein Kampf* as a lesson in genius nation-building.

These encounters with the Jewish experience meant that I did not bring to Israel my Tagore-educated suspicion of nationalism. I saw exigencies in the creation of a Jewish state: the exodus of Jewish survivors from a Europe where they were not wanted, the rapid British abandonment of their rule over Palestine, and the UN's declaration of a two-state solution. Long after the picture of Moshe Dayan came down from my bedroom wall, I did not cease to see Israel the way its leaders had from the 1960s begun to present the country: as redemption for the victims of the Shoah, and an unbreakable guarantee against its recurrence.

Personal encounters with Palestinian students at the Indian universities I attended, and readings in Ghassan Kanafani, Mourid Barghouti, Emile Habibi, Raja Shehadeh and Ghada Karmi, had also simultaneously convinced me of the justice of the Palestinian cause. I learned about how Zionists achieved a Jewish majority through systematic ethnic cleansing of the Arab-inhabited areas of Palestine and their theft of Palestinian land and property. As I learned about the squalid, barely examined and often actively suppressed history of the Nakba, and of subsequent massacres and expulsions of Palestinians, I recognised a terrible imbalance of cultural prestige and power between Israeli Jews and Palestinian Arabs. My own early kinship with the off-modern Jewish sensibility and indifference to Palestinian fates attested to the mordant truth of Edward Said's words in *After the Last Sky* (1986): 'we have no known Einsteins, no Chagall, no Freud or Rubinstein to protect us with a legacy of glorious achievements'.

The acrimonious spats between Arab students from Libya, Jordan, Iraq and Syria on my university campus in Delhi in the early 1990s, as Yasser Arafat stood in solidarity with Saddam Hussein, revealed how Palestinians were also disadvantaged by their lack of effective leaders and allies against internationally connected and resourceful Zionists. I could see, too, the insidious racism that had helped prioritise the interests of the West's chosen nation in the Middle East while demeaning Palestinian suffering in Western eyes. Mohammad Tarbush points out unarguably in his memoir *My Palestine* (2024) that Palestinians 'were ethnically cleansed from Palestine not only because we were the weaker party in a power game but because we were perceived as non-entities whose aspirations for a dignified life were beneath consideration'.

I still found it hard to resist the Zionist logic: that Jews cannot survive in non-Jewish lands and must have a state of their own and should never be reduced to a minority in it, exposed again to persecution. I was aware, more than the most well-educated people I knew in India, how little the plight of Jews scapegoated during Germany's social and economic breakdown in the 1920s and 30s had registered in the conscience of Western European and American leaders, that even Shoah survivors were met with a cold shoulder, and, in Eastern Europe, with fresh pogroms. And so, a part of me could still explain away Zionist violence against local Palestinian fighters and invading Arab armies, the expulsion of hundreds of thousands of Palestinians, the occupation of their lands and homes, and the destruction of Palestinian identities of Arab villages and towns.

Similar, and much worse, atrocities had, after all, occurred during and after the partition of British-ruled India, when more than 15 million people moved across new borders, and hundreds of thousands of women were raped or abducted amid a frenzy that filled trains with corpses, and clogged canals, roads and tracks with dismembered bodies. While during and after the war, Allied powers had mercilessly supervised the expulsion of more than 12 million Germans from Central and Eastern Europe. The history of the modern world showed that violence was, more often than not, the midwife of nation states, and most of its victims were innocent.

Besides, for Jews in Palestine, more than for Indians, Pakistanis, Indonesians and the Vietnamese, a nation of their own was a matter of life or death, after their very recent experience of racially motivated mass murder. I even thought it was unjust that Israel alone among all the countries in the world needed to justify its right to exist. And I privately recoiled when friends and acquaintances in the media grew rancorous in their criticisms of Israel, blaming their inability to express them publicly on Jews in prominent positions.

I wasn't so naive to think that suffering ennobles or empowers the victims of a great atrocity to act in a morally superior way. Dalits in India, probably the largest continuously persecuted group in history, had joined their upper-caste tormentors in killing and raping Muslims during the pogrom supervised by Narendra Modi in the state of Gujarat in 2002. Jews of Middle Eastern origin, once subject to racial abuse and discrimination by an Israeli ruling class of European ancestry, now dictated the terms of humiliation to Palestinians. Jabotinsky himself had mocked the liberal humanist assumption according to which 'anyone who has himself suffered for a long time under the yoke of a stronger one will not oppress those weaker than he'. That yesterday's victims are very likely to become today's victimisers is the lesson of organised violence in the former Yugoslavia, Sudan, Congo, Rwanda, Sri Lanka, Afghanistan and too many other places. I was still shocked by the dark meaning the Israeli state had drawn from the Shoah, and then institutionalised in a machinery of repression.

*

Back in 2008, the far-right movement that began to establish Jewish settlements in Gaza and the West Bank during the 1970s had yet to monopolise political power in Israel. The country's politics had begun to move to the right after the second Palestinian intifada (2000–5) – a shift accelerated by Jewish voters of Middle Eastern ancestry who not only formed a solid core of support for Likud, but also came to dominate political discourse and culture. But the ideas of Meir Kahane, a rabbi from Flatbush, Brooklyn, who urged the Israeli government to form a 'Jewish terrorist group' that would 'throw bombs and grenades to kill Arabs' and encouraged Jews to buy .22 calibre weapons – 'Every Jew a .22' – were not in the mainstream. Men like Israel's minister of national security Itamar Ben-Gvir, convicted multiple times (including for incitement of racism and support-ing a terrorist organisation), were far from becoming senior cabinet ministers and public advocates of mass extermination of Palestinians from their high perches. Nevertheless, I could detect a certain hardening of tone in private conversations.

I had been struck, reading *A Tale of Love and Darkness* (2002), Amos Oz's memoir of his childhood in Jeru-salem in the 1940s and 50s, by how Arabs had barely existed in the eyes of Israel's foremost writer. In *Once Upon a Country* (2007), Sari Nusseibeh, who had grown up in East Jerusalem about a hundred feet away from Oz, remarks on this absence, explaining that it 'wasn't a product of malevolence or ill will . . . Uppermost in the Jews' mind were the Nazi death camps they had narrowly escaped,' he wrote. From what I had seen in the late 2000s, attitudes towards Arabs seemed to have moved from unconcern to active contempt.

Those in Israel's small and beleaguered human rights community confessed to a disquiet about the moral decay of their society. The deepening rot was manifest in the summer of 2024 in the spectacle of Israeli mobs storming two military bases to protest soldiers being detained for sexually abusing Palestinians. Already in 2008, the targeted killings of Palestinians, checkpoints, home demolitions, land thefts, arbitrary and indefinite detentions, and widespread torture in prisons seemed to proclaim a pitiless national ethos: that humankind is divided into those who are strong and those who are weak, and so those who have been or expect to be victims should pre-emptively crush their perceived enemies.

In 2000 I had published a series of articles in the *New York Review of Books* on the valley of Kashmir, where India's military occupation had consumed tens of thousands of lives. That same year I had gone to Pakistan and Afghanistan to report on the upsurges of Islamic fanaticism there. In 2002, I had written about the killing of more than two thousand Muslims in a pogrom supervised by Narendra Modi in the western Indian state of Gujarat. I had monitored in several subsequent articles and books

India's descent from being the world's largest democracy to being potentially its first Hindu ethnonational state. I knew how quickly a country could lose the glow of heroic virtue given by its founding fathers, whether Nehru and Gandhi, or Herzl and Chaim Weizmann, the first president of Israel, and the ceremony of routine elections. I had witnessed, too, the undermining of an entire people and culture in Tibet by an explicitly authoritarian regime.

Still, nothing prepared me for the brutality and squalor of Israel's occupation: the snaking wall and numerous roadblocks in the West Bank meant to torment Palestinians in their own land, separating them from their place of work, their relatives and neighbours, and children from their schools, and the racially exclusive network of shiny asphalt roads, electricity grids and water systems linking the illegal Jewish settlements to Israel. Even Joe Sacco's graphic novel *Palestine* (1993), probably the most vivid account of the structures and mentalities of oppression in the West Bank and Gaza, hadn't primed me for the sadistic gratification drawn by the settlers, often with American accents, in shooting Palestinian villagers, and destroying their cars, homes, farms and water tanks. I had read with mounting outrage about the degradation of Palestinians, during successive military assaults on the West Bank and Gaza, turning them into laboratory rats for the testing of high-tech weaponry and surveillance systems that Israel sold around the world. Yet nothing in the scholarship about the

Israeli occupation matched the experience of witnessing its profit motive in action: the plunder of Palestinian
natural resources by Israeli companies, their flooding of
Palestinian markets with made-in-Israel goods, and their
exploitation of low-wage Palestinian labour.

Nor had anything I read in Edward Said or Noam
Chomsky prepared me to discover, for myself, how
insidiously Israel's high-placed supporters in the West
conceal the nihilistic survival-of-the-strongest ideology
reproduced by all Israeli regimes. Like many writers and
journalists exposed to Israel's occupation for the first
time, I returned with an awakened, affronted sensibility.
But my own efforts to write about it for the American
publications I contributed to went nowhere. I had already
noticed the near-total exclusion of Palestinian and Arab
voices from them. The demurrals from editors, which
were couched diplomatically, implying that a writer from
India on this subject lacked credentials, made me more
aware of a resolute regime of pre-censorship in even
liberal periodicals. As for the suffering of the dispossessed and dehumanised Palestinians, it passed without
much scrutiny. Those calling attention to the spectacle
of Washington's blind commitment to Israel risked
inviting a potentially destructive charge of antisemitism.

It was now clear to me that Israel did not, as Dorothy
Thompson pointed out in 1951, 'live in the same atmos-
phere of free criticism which every other state in the
world must endure'. Demoralised by my failure to write

about the country, I understood Thompson instinctively when she wrote, 'people don't like to be craven and mealy-mouthed: every time one yields to such pressure, one is filled with self-contempt and this self-contempt works itself out in resentment of those who caused it'.

The combination of external suppression and aggrieved self-censorship meant that year after year the accumulating ironies of Israel went unnoticed: how after promising safety to Jews worldwide, the Israeli government raised alarms routinely about their imminent destruction; how while claiming Zionism as a guarantee of Jewish self-sufficiency and protection against antisemitism, Israel had become utterly reliant upon foreign military hardware in its struggles against its neighbours and the support of American antisemitic evangelicals, who trusted the return of the Jews to the Holy Land would bring about Armageddon. And how, while effectively instrumentalising the Nazi genocide, Israel had started to collaborate with Turkish governments to deny the Armenians the right to describe as genocide the murder of hundreds of thousands in Anatolia by the Ottoman Empire in 1915–16.*

*

* In *Sultanic Saviors and Tolerant Turks* (2020), the historian Marc David Baer demonstrates how prominent historians of the Ottoman Empire, including Bernard Lewis, joined the Turkish government, major Jewish American organisations and the State of Israel in suppressing the Armenian genocide.

For months after my trip to Israel in 2008, I lived with a strange disturbance, unlike any I had known after visiting other atrocity sites, where individuals had also been executed in broad daylight, children brutalised by vengeful soldiers, houses bulldozed or burned, and families shattered by imprisonment and torture of their loved ones. The Palestinians under occupation stood so far apart from their persecutors; and I found it unnerving, too, that their persecutors were the West's former victims who now possessed the ease and safety of a Western lifestyle on both sides of the wall dividing Israel from the West Bank.

Perhaps my heart would also have shrivelled had I witnessed the degradations of racist imperialism in South Africa, the great abyss yawning between a white ruling class armed by Western powers and the destitute black population. In any case, the gap between the young beach revellers in Tel Aviv, or the settler lounging by his hilltop swimming pool, and the inhabitants of Palestinian slum towns was too great. And despite my indebtedness to Jewish thinkers and artists, and my self-image as a person not swayed by sectarian sentiments, here was a resemblance I could not deny: the Palestinians – the hijab-clad grandmother kneeling in the dust before an Ashkenazi teenager with an Uzi, or the eager aspiring writers at Birzeit University – were people who looked like me, and who now endured a nightmare that I and my own ancestors had put behind us.

Once seen and piercingly recognised, they could not be forgotten; transfixed in my imagination as individuals close to me in every way, compatriots, in whose presence I saw a reproach of living comfortably while they were suffering, they could not be reduced to an anonymous mass of victims, or distant objects of pity and guilt. I felt inescapably implicated in their plight. Just as the Shoah seemed uniquely abhorrent to many for being perpetrated in the heart of Western civilisation, so did to me the abuse of Palestinians by Jewish Israelis as late as the twenty-first century, decades after the formal end of the West's regime of racist colonialism.

I felt a bit foolish, too, over how little I had known about Israel, and resentful of the Western politicians and journalists who had kept up for so long the pretence of a 'peace process' and a 'two-state solution' (and turned away when Palestinians, taking their patronising advice, embraced non-violent civil resistance and, as happened over the course of eighteen months during the Great March of Return, were repeatedly massacred). Writing in 1982, the French Jewish historian Pierre Vidal-Naquet, whose parents were murdered during the war, had already seen what was only now becoming obvious to me (and still remains concealed from many): that for successive Israeli governments, 'it is not a question and it never seriously has been a question of letting Israel *and* Palestine coexist. Instead, these governments have posed an alternative: Israel *or* Palestine.' Israeli policy has tried, Vidal-Naquet stressed, 'to *erase* Palestine'.

In reading and annotating the writings of Améry, Levi, Bauman and others, I was trying somehow to mitigate the oppressive sense of wrongness I felt after being exposed to Israel's construal of the Shoah: its nationalisation of the ruthless principle that only those who are strong and strike first deserve to live. The confusion I had felt reading Gitta Sereny's book about Jewish survivors in Treblinka after watching *Schindler's List* became more oppressive. Was the country's elevation, to resounding approbation from Western powers, of survival into the sole value and purpose of human life the main lesson of the Shoah? If so, what distinguished the legacy of the Shoah from nineteenth-century social Darwinism – the toxic core of European nationalisms and imperialisms (including Germany's) competing for *Lebensraum*?

In Améry, Levi and other survivors I was looking for a different, more exalted, or at least less bleak, meaning of the Shoah, and some reassurance from people who had known, in their own frail bodies, the monstrous terror visited on millions by a supposedly civilised European nation state – people who knew what it meant to be excluded, persecuted and murdered, and who had resolved to be on perpetual guard against the deformation of the Shoah's meaning and the abuse of its memory. But there was no reassurance to be found in their writings, or in their lives after the Shoah, which with all their redemptive feats of understanding they had finally found unbearable and chosen to end.

'The triumph of human identity and worth over the pathology of human destruction glows virtually everywhere in Levi's writing,' Toni Morrison wrote in her introduction to a three-volume collection of Levi's works. It was also the moral I wanted to draw from his work. But there were no uplifting messages in Levi's vision of an irredeemable and lasting human degradation. A film like *Schindler's List* offered a brief solace with its peculiarly American vision, in which adversity elicits moral courage and feats of heroism from ordinary individuals, and the human spirit ultimately triumphs (for some survivors, at least). Oskar Schindler and the more than 28,000 people who saved Jews during the Shoah – celebrated by Yad Vashem as the Righteous among the Nations – spoke of the persistence of valour and decency among a minuscule minority. But no redeeming truth could be drawn, outside schlocky movies and state propaganda memorials celebrating survival, rescue and resistance, from the unlimited cruelty of six million murders. Rather, it seemed as if such an evil as the Shoah could not but have a long spectral presence in the lives of individuals and societies.

Levi himself had started to feel immediately after his

liberation from Auschwitz that however hard he and
fellow inmates tried to 'wash from our consciences and
our memories the monstrosity that lay there', nothing
would ever be 'good and pure enough to wipe out our
past, and that the marks of the offense would remain
in us forever, and in the memories of those who were
present, and in the places where it happened, and in the
stories that we would make of it'. Already on his long
journey back to Italy, during which he met young Zionists heading for Palestine, Levi could sense 'the incurable
nature of the offense, which spreads like an infection'.
He ultimately saw the Shoah as 'an inexhaustible source
of evil' which 'is perpetuated as hatred in the survivors,
and springs up in a thousand ways, against the very will
of all, as a thirst for revenge, as moral breakdown, as
negation, as weariness, as resignation'.

Levi's warning, and his writings in general, became
a touchstone as I started to learn about the most dramatic turnaround in Jewish history: the propelling of
a small minority from a marginal, passive and despised
existence in the West into the very heart of the modern
world, complicit in almost all its fateful developments
and historic antagonisms.

I had seen Israel grounded in an urgent moral and
existential necessity after the Shoah. Yet the pathologies of survivalist nationalism had already infected the
Yishuv, the pre-state Jewish community in Palestine.

Hans Kohn, an early Zionist and the pioneering scholar of nationalism, who lived in Palestine for nine years, saw them from up close. In 1928, after two Arabs had just been murdered outside his home in Jerusalem, Kohn complained in a letter to a friend that '95 percent of the Yishuv supports such murders': 'We have degenerated in a horrible way due to our nationalism . . . Who can afford to be a part of this? Just like in the world war, each barbarity, like this barbarity, is presented as a necessity.' In May 1948, Kohn, a founding member of the Brit Shalom circle of German Jewish intellectuals working for peaceful coexistence of Jews and Arabs in Palestine, wrote to the American Jewish Committee (he was a member of its executive board) to warn against the 'extreme ruthlessness of the Zionist armed forces' who might 'succeed in expelling or annihilating most of the Palestinian Arabs'.

In a letter to the philosopher Gershom Scholem in 1946, Arendt was convinced that 'there is a very real danger that a consistent nationalist has no other choice but to become a racist' and that 'the metamorphosis of a people into a racial horde is an ever-present danger in our times . . . I strongly believe that a Jewish nation-state would be a stupid and dangerous game.' Arendt's dire prophecy was realised in many other countries, including my own. It was also true that from 'remorselessly accumulating cemeteries', as Benedict Anderson wrote in *Imagined Communities* (1983), 'the nation's biography snatches exemplary suicides, poignant martyrdoms, assassinations, executions, wars and holocausts' and that 'to serve the narrative purpose, these violent deaths must be remembered/forgotten as "our own"'.

War memorials in Europe's remotest villages, as well as the cemeteries of Normandy, Verdun, the Marne, Passchendaele, Reichswald and the Somme enshrine the continent's extensive experience of bereavement in two world wars. Commemorations of the more than 20 million dead in the Great Patriotic War serve a unifying purpose as much in the Russian Federation as they did in the former Soviet Union. Still, as I discovered, there was something unprecedented about how Israel had forged a collective memory of death and trauma, and used it to shape national identity and culture, while also deploying it to devastating military and geopolitical effect.

'Israel today is becoming Yad Vashem with an air force,' Thomas Friedman noted with alarm in 1989, in his book *From Beirut to Jerusalem*; he hoped that 'the "Holocausting" of the Israeli psyche' was still reversible with 'proper and healthy leadership'. By 2008, the Shoah seemed everywhere in Israel, if not in the presence of actual victims, most of whom were dead or dying, then in the paranoia of its rulers and publicists, in works of literature, textbooks, monuments, gravestone inscriptions and state-sponsored school trips to Auschwitz. And it became apparent as I explored further that this national consciousness was not a perfectly natural entity, springing from a traumatic event. Rather, it emerged out of a battle between different outlooks and interests, against a backdrop of changing sociopolitical realities and intense struggles for power. Like any ideological formation, the discourse of the Shoah had to be traced back to the time and place where it was first outlined, disseminated and consumed.

Raul Hilberg, author of the monumental study *The Destruction of the European Jews* (1961), remembers thinking in the 1960s that 'interest in the Holocaust was gone permanently'. Indeed, he had found it very difficult to find a publisher for his path-breaking book. 'But in 1975 or so,' he adds, 'the picture changed entirely.' It is strange to recall today, when the Shoah is the essential component of 'Israeliness' and 'Jewishness', that for many years there was in Israel, as well as in Europe and the United States, 'no space in the public sphere for the history of the Holocaust or for the bearers of its direct memory – the survivors'. As Idith Zertal writes in *Israel's Holocaust and the Politics of Nationhood* (2005), 'acts of commemoration, were few and sporadic . . . In a 220-page textbook of Jewish history published in 1948, only one page was devoted to the Holocaust, compared to ten pages on the Napoleonic wars.'

The memorial and documentation centre Yad Vashem

is at the centre of Israel's pedagogical efforts today. Back in the 1940s, the government actively worked to postpone 'the establishment of an official, government-sponsored institution to cultivate the memory of the Holocaust and its victims'. More astoundingly, survivors were drenched with contempt by the leaders of the Zionist movement as well as unrepentant antisemites. George S. Patton, the American general in charge of the single largest population of Jewish displaced persons (DPs) after the war, described them as a 'sub-human species'. The first prime minister of Israel, as we have seen, concurred.

The Israeli-Irish writer Ronit Lentin remembers in her book *Israel and the Daughters of the Shoah* (2000) how she was trained to despise diaspora Jews for having 'gone passively to their death'. Jewish diaspora life was seen, she writes, 'as doomed to destruction and Zionism as the only answer to the plight of the Jewish people'. Israel, she recalls, 'was the place where Jews would be proud again, would take up arms to fight their "enemies"', and would never again 'go to their death like lambs to the slaughter'. The Shoah's victims were feminised in contradistinction to the image of the Israeli sabra, depicted as a young male soldier with blond hair and blue eyes fighting for his country, like Paul Newman in *Exodus* (1960). Many Zionists, like Hindu nationalists, had internalised the racist arraignment from Christian

Europeans that their co-religionists were cowards and weaklings; they worked hard to show themselves replete with the masculine virtues of strength and valour, especially as evidence of what they despised as weakness continued to pile up.

Unaware of what their persecutors were planning, some Jews had helped the Nazis, much, as Hannah Arendt wrote, to the latter's surprise. Jewish community leaders 'could be trusted to compile the lists of persons and of their property, to secure money from the deportees to defray the expenses of their deportation and extermination, to keep track of vacated apartments, to supply police forces to help seize Jews and get them on trains'. 'The role of the Jewish leaders in the destruction of their own people', in Arendt's severe verdict, was 'undoubtedly the darkest chapter of the whole dark story'.

Arendt's account of passive compliance by Jewish leaders in Europe – and more generally her denial that antisemitism alone was to blame for the Shoah and her emphasis on the innate genocidal potential of the modern bureaucratic state – incited rancorous attacks on her from Israeli authorities and intellectuals. For early historical accounts of the Jewish state had privileged heroic myths constructed around anti-Nazi resistance in Europe, especially the Warsaw uprising in 1943. 'Basically,' Raul Hilberg wrote, 'there had been no meaningful resistance' – a truth for which, Hilberg noted, he and a couple of other writers, including Arendt, were pilloried in Israel.*

No Zionists living in Palestine helped, or could help, the ghetto uprising in Warsaw. Nevertheless, in 1951, Israel established the Holocaust Remembrance Day to mark the anniversary of the uprising. And the ragtag band of rebels in Warsaw, who had been socialists and communists and members of the secular socialist Bund as well as Zionists, were cast as the avatars of the vigorous and muscular 'New Jews' making Israel, their heroic memory serving as an antidote to the awareness that the large majority of the Jewish people seemed to have gone, unresisting, to their death.

During this collective emotional makeover in the 1950s, a madly intense search for Jewish partners of Nazis was launched. Israel Kastner, one of the leaders of Hungarian Jewry who had helped Jews escape from occupied Europe, was indicted for collaborating with Adolf Eichmann. After a trial, where the judge accused him of selling his soul to the devil, Kastner was assassinated in 1957 by far-right zealots, a year before he was finally acquitted by Israel's Supreme Court.

More such national self-purgings occurred as Zionists who had lived relatively safely in Palestine throughout the Shoah prosecuted dozens of Jews forced to make

---

* There had been no meaningful resistance from the millions of Soviet prisoners of war, either; the Nazi regime had rendered it impossible.

terrible choices while exposed to extreme violence and terror in Europe. These were, Idith Zertal points out, 'individuals trapped in insoluble dilemmas with no way out except suicide; who, for one brief moment outside of "normal" time, turned into persecutors, beating, slapping, whipping, and torturing other people for more food, less work, less suffering, to save themselves'. She quotes Primo Levi's stern words on the subject of collaborators: 'no one is authorized to judge them, not those who lived through the experience of the Lager and even less those who did not'. Levi, who had become reconciled to the inevitability of human failings in everyone, including himself, did not have much patience with the demand for moral perfection.*

As it happened, Zertal writes, 'not *one* of the defendants tried under the law was charged with or found guilty of directly or indirectly causing the death of a single person'. But then those drawing the hyper-masculine image of the new Jewish state wished to avoid knowledge of the moral universe created by Nazi terror in which Jews were coerced into becoming persecutors, reluctant accomplices to their own destruction. The makers of nationalism in a society fighting for territory

---

* In *Hope Against Hope* (1970), her account of the regime of persecution and murder under Stalin, Nadezhda Mandelstam raises an unanswerable question: 'Why are we supposed to be brave enough to stand up to all the horrors of twentieth-century prisons and camps?'

and demanding from its young a commitment to self-sacrifice were forging an ideologically pure self-image. Thus, not only the collaborators, but also Marek Edelman, the celebrated commander of the Warsaw uprising, who depicted armed resistance in much less heroic terms (and also criticised Israel), were almost erased from the official narrative of the Shoah.*

But it was the prosecution of not Kastner and other Jewish 'collaborators' but of a Nazi war criminal that accelerated the conversion of the victims and survivors of the Shoah into ideological and political arguments in the service of Zionism. The tone was set in the very first statement by the main prosecutor, Attorney General Gideon Hausner, at the trial of Adolf Eichmann in 1961:

> When I stand before you here, Judges of Israel, to lead the prosecution of Adolf Eichmann, I am not standing alone. With me are six million accusers. But they cannot rise to their feet and point an accusing finger towards him who sits in the dock and cry: 'I accuse.' For their ashes are piled up on the hills of Auschwitz

---

* Edelman rejected the idea that Israel was an inheritor of the Shoah. In an interview with a Polish journalist, he said: 'Israel is a chauvinist, religious state, where a Christian is a second-class citizen and a Muslim is third-class. It is a disaster, after three million were murdered in Poland, they want to dominate everything and not to consider non-Jews!'

and the fields of Treblinka, and are strewn in the for-
ests of Poland. Their graves are scattered throughout
the length and breadth of Europe. Their blood cries
out, but their voice is not heard. Therefore I will be
their spokesman and in their name I will unfold this
terrible indictment.

For the next four months, witnesses recounted not only
the depravities of the death camps but also the heroism
of Jewish resisters, particularly the Zionists of Israeli
imagination who led the uprising in the Warsaw Ghetto
(Edelman was not mentioned). Broadcast live on radio,
the indictment of Adolf Eichmann in Jerusalem by
an Israeli court 'changed', as Zertal writes, 'the face of
Israel, psychologically binding the pastless young Israelis
with their recent history and revolutionizing their self-
perception' beside shaping a 'western post-Holocaust
culture and the effort to grapple with [its] history and
memory'.

Eichmann was sentenced to death at the end of 1961
and executed six months later. But his trial aimed not so
much at establishing his guilt (obvious) for monstrous
crimes (fundamentally unpunishable) as at changing
domestic and world opinion. The effect on Israeli self-
perceptions was immediate and revolutionary: 'Only the
Jewish state can now defend Jewish blood,' declared an
editorial in *Yedioth Ahronoth* in a special edition of the

Hebrew newspaper published a few hours after Ben-Gurion announced to the Knesset that Eichmann had been arrested and would be tried in Israel:

> The capture of the Nazi exterminator by the remnants of the exterminated people and his judgment by a Jewish tribunal according to Jewish justice is meant to prove to terrorists of all kinds, Germans and non-Germans, brown, white, red, black and all those who have already prepared themselves for the role of future exterminators of Jews, that Jewish blood will never be defenseless again.

Writing to Karl Jaspers before she travelled to Jerusalem, Arendt was convinced that the trial was 'an effort to show Israeli youth and (worse yet) the whole world certain things. Among others, that Jews who aren't Israelis will wind up in situations where they will let themselves be slaughtered like sheep. Also: that the Arabs were hand in glove with the Nazis. There are other possibilities for distorting the issue itself.'

All these predictions turned out to be true. Ben-Gurion, who had secretly ordered Eichmann's abduction in Argentina and also stage-managed his trial, did aim to present Israel as the defender of all Jews. He also hoped to publicise internationally the Israeli conflation of Arabs with Nazis. In an interview with the *New York*

Times, Ben-Gurion hoped that 'the Eichmann trial will help to ferret out other Nazis – for example, the connection between Nazis and some Arab rulers'.

This idea that Nazis are always present among us, especially among Arabs, was the beginning of an enduring trend in Israeli nationalist narratives. The Palestinian Mufti of Jerusalem, Haj Amin al-Husseini, an antisemitic megalomaniac who delusionally promised mass Muslim support to the Nazis,* is depicted in the Israeli-produced *Encyclopedia of the Holocaust* (1990), in an entry that is almost as long as that on Hitler, as one of the major designers and perpetrators of the Final Solution. In a speech to the World Zionist Congress in Jerusalem in 2015, Netanyahu claimed that it was al-Husseini who persuaded a dithering Hitler to proceed and 'burn' the Jews.

Ben-Gurion hoped that the move to finger the new Nazis in Arab countries would obscure the responsibility of the true perpetrators of the Shoah then still living under official protection in West Germany – the country from which he had just secured much cash and weapons. Ben-Gurion, claiming that 'we don't want the Arab

---

* One of Gandhi's colleagues, Subhas Chandra Bose, also offered his services to Hitler in 1941, and went on to assist the Japanese invasion of British India; he is one of the most revered nationalist icons of India today. The notion that my enemy's enemy is my friend also motivated the Jewish militant leader Avraham Stern to try, in 1940, to enlist Nazi support against the British rulers of Palestine.

Nazis to come and slaughter us', also wanted to present Israel as yet again threatened with a Shoah, and so obliged to protect itself by any means necessary, including nuclear bombs. Writing a seven-page letter to US president John F. Kennedy in the spring of 1963, in an attempt to justify Israel's nuclear programme, he argued that the 'liberation of Palestine' is 'impossible without the total destruction of the people in Israel'.

The trial of Eichmann and the fresh focus on the Shoah also served to nation-build at home. By the early 1960s, the Shoah seemed the safest, and least controversial, basis for a collective Israeli identity. Immigrants from Arab countries had come to constitute a majority in a society previously conceived of as almost exclusively European. Ben-Gurion had never expected this demographic setback. It was only after 1945 that he realised that in order to proclaim a Jewish state in Palestine with a Jewish majority he had to quickly implement a plan wholly alien to the original Zionist programme: to deliver all the Jews, numbering over a million, from Arab countries to Palestine. He now hoped to educate the so-called Oriental Jews, some of whom were sprayed with insecticide when they arrived in the Promised Land, about the Shoah and European antisemitism (neither of which they were familiar with) and start binding them with Jews of European ancestry in what seemed all too clearly an imperfectly imagined community.

*

In *The Seventh Million*, Tom Segev recounts how Begin, who had accused his bitter rival Ben-Gurion of insensitivity to Shoah survivors, advanced this process of forging a Shoah consciousness among darker-skinned Jews who had long been the target of racist humiliations by the country's white establishment. Begin healed their injuries of class and race by promising them stolen Palestinian land and a socio-economic status above dispossessed and destitute Arabs.

Moshe Dayan defined another, equally enduring, consequence of the trial. 'There can be no doubt that only this country and only this people can protect the Jews against a second Holocaust. And hence every inch of Israeli soil is intended only for Jews.' In other words, Israel's right to exist as an ethnonational state, exerted in perpetuity against Palestinian claims, safeguarded the right of Jews in the diaspora to live without fear of another Shoah.

This kind of rhetoric became more prevalent in the spring of 1967 when Israeli and many diaspora Jews came to perceive themselves, while weirdly oblivious to the reality of Israeli military supremacy in the Middle East, as threatened by another Shoah. The exterminationist bombast of Egyptian president Nasser was plainly not matched by his capability. The Israeli leaders knew it. So did the US president Lyndon B. Johnson. 'All of our intelligence people are unanimous,' Johnson told Abba Eban on 26 May, 'you will whip hell out of them.'

As it happened, striking pre-emptively, the Israel Defense Forces under Dayan crushed its manifold Arab enemies in six days. But the trial of Eichmann, and the renovated national narrative of the Shoah, meant that Nazis plotting another Shoah would always seem to lurk at the gates of Israel. The 'perpetual Israeli condition', Zertal writes, would now be that 'of a lone, beleaguered nation surrounded by an antagonistic, anti-Semitic world, and that of the eternal victim'.

Possession of the sites of Jewish scripture in the newly occupied territories reinforced the millenarian dimension to Israel's narrative. Returning from a visit to the Western Wall in the Arab sector of Jerusalem, barely a week after the end of the war, Elie Wiesel claimed that 'even the free thinkers among us talk about an experience that is in its essence religious'. Within a few months, settlers were moving into the occupied territories with the consent and assistance of the Israelis' secular leadership. No less than the moderate Abba Eban was arguing that withdrawal from the occupied territories would be a return to 'Auschwitz borders'. Begin would invoke the same bogey of imminent genocide to invade Lebanon in 1982.

It took some time for outsiders to notice the moral degradations wrought by the new discourse among both Israelis and their American supporters. One notably unexpected and bewildered reaction came from Woody Allen. 'I am appalled beyond measure by the treatment of the rioting Palestinians by the Jews,' he wrote in a *New York Times* op-ed in January 1988 after Israeli defence minister Yitzhak Rabin, responding to the Palestinian intifada in the occupied territories in 1987, ordered the army enforce an 'iron fist policy', which included firing live ammunition at stone-throwing protesters and breaking their bones.* 'Breaking the hands of men and women so they can't throw stones?' Allen marvelled. 'Am I reading the newspapers correctly? . . . Are we talking about state-sanctioned brutality and even torture? My goodness!' The following month, four of the most prominent Israeli writers, Yehuda Amichai, Amos Elon, Amos Oz and A. B. Yehoshua, published a letter in the *New York Times* imploring more American Jews to 'speak up'. In cleaving to the common wisdom to 'keep quiet' and 'support whatever Israeli government happens to be in power', American Jews were 'massively intervening in Israeli politics and silently but effectively supporting one side in the debate, the tragically wrong side'.

But the wrong side possessed the most emotionally compelling argument. In March 1988, Yehuda Elkana, director of the Van Leer Institute and later president of Central European University, urged his compatriots in a much-discussed article in *Haaretz* to forget the Shoah. Elkana, deported to Auschwitz at the age of ten, blamed

---

* In 1991, Allen recalled his amazement 'at how many intellectuals took issue' with him over his piece.

the brutishness of the Israeli occupation on a 'profound existential "Angst"' fed by the privatisation of the Shoah and by a willingness to 'believe that the whole world is against us and that we are the eternal victim'. 'It may be that it is important for the world at large to remember' the Shoah, he wrote, but Israelis 'must learn to forget'.

It was too late. The Israeli far right soon began to describe a nascent peace process with Palestinians advanced by Yitzhak Rabin after the intifada as a prologue to Jewish annihilation. The hawkish general turned peacemaker and his foreign minister, Shimon Peres, were depicted as members of the Judenrat and Kapos, the Nazi-appointed Jewish leaders who had helped in the administration of the death camps. Posters at anti-Oslo demonstrations, where Netanyahu often spoke, portrayed Rabin wearing an SS uniform – the ideological prelude to his assassination in 1995, and irreversible injury to the possibility of a large 'peace' camp in Israeli politics.

Mobs supporting the rapists of a Palestinian prisoner, or blocking food supplies to Gaza, present a new face of Israel today to many of its supporters. Yeshayahu Leibowitz was already warning in 1986, even before Israel ruthlessly crushed the first intifada, that 'if the present situation continues ... the growing savagery of Israeli society will be as inevitable as the severance of the state from the Jews of the world'. Leibowitz predicted that

Israeli policy would 'end in mass expulsion and slaughter of the Arab population', which would 'lead to a decisive war between Israel and the Arab world':

> In that war the sympathy and backing of the entire world will be for the Arabs. Already today, the state of Israel, to which most of the world's nations were once sympathetic, has earned contempt and hatred throughout the world. Its very existence has come to depend on a thin life-line stretching out to it from the White House. Above all, the state, which was to have been the pride and glory of the Jewish people, is rapidly becoming an embarrassment to it.

This has never seemed truer than today when the Israeli military, using the arsenal of Western democracies, has massacred and starved Palestinians, razed their homes, schools, hospitals, mosques, churches, bombed them into smaller and smaller encampments, while denouncing as antisemitic or champions of Hamas all those who plead with it to desist, from the United Nations, Amnesty International and Human Rights Watch to the Spanish, Irish, Brazilian and South African governments and the Vatican.

Recklessly identifying criticism of Israel's conduct with antisemitism, Israeli propagandists have helped spread anti-Jewish sentiment around the world. Israel's most devout friends have then further inflamed this situation. The earliest of them, Dorothy Thompson, was warning American Jews by the end of the 1940s against 'Zionist propaganda', specifically 'the claim that every Jew in the world is, by his very existence, a member of the Jewish "nation", from which he cannot and may not extricate himself'. It is a claim, she wrote in *Commentary* in March 1950, 'never before made, to my recollection, by anybody except anti-Semites'. Biden, nevertheless, kept making the very same argument while questioning Palestinian casualty figures and invoking non-existent atrocity videos: that the safety of the Jewish population worldwide depends on Israel. 'If there weren't an Israel,' he was still saying in July 2024, days before being discarded as a political liability by his own party, 'every Jew in the world would be at risk.'

The *New York Times* columnist Ezra Klein took a more commonsensical view during the Israeli war on Gaza: 'Do I feel safer? Do I feel like there's less antisemitism in the world right now because of what is happening there, or does it seem to me that there's a huge upsurge of antisemitism, and that even Jews in places that are not Israel are vulnerable to what happens in Israel?' This ruinous scenario was very clearly anticipated by many Shoah survivors. Bauman warned repeatedly after the 1980s that such tactics by unscrupulous politicians like Begin and Netanyahu were securing 'a post-mortem triumph for Hitler, who dreamed of creating conflict between Jews and the whole world' and 'preventing Jews from ever having peaceful coexistence with others'. Jean Améry, made desperate in his last years by 'burgeoning antisemitism', pleaded with Israelis to treat even Palestinian terrorists humanely, so that the solidarity between diaspora Zionists like himself and Israel did not 'become the basis for a communion of two doomed parties in the face of catastrophe'.

There isn't much to be hoped for in this regard from Israel's present leaders. The discovery of their extreme vulnerability and isolation should make them more willing to risk a compromise peace settlement. Yet, with all the weaponry lavished on them by the United States, they seek to further militarise their occupation of the West Bank and Gaza, and to provoke their enemies in Yemen, Lebanon and Iran into an ever wider war. Such is the long-term damage Boaz Evron feared when he warned against 'the continuous mentioning of the Holocaust, antisemitism and the hatred of Jews in all generations'. 'A leadership cannot be separated from its own propaganda,' he wrote, and Israel's ruling class act like the chieftains of a 'sect' operating 'in the world of myths and monsters created by its own hands', 'no longer able to understand what is happening in the real world' or the 'historical processes in which the state is caught'.

More than four decades after Evron wrote this, it is clearer, too, that Israel's Western patrons have turned out to be among the country's worst enemies, ushering their ward deeper into hallucination. As Evron said, Western powers act against their 'own interests and apply to

Israel a special preferential relationship, without Israel seeing itself obligated to reciprocate'. Consequently, 'the special treatment given to Israel, expressed in unconditional economic and political support' has 'created an economic and political hothouse around Israel cutting it off from global economic and political realities'.

With Israel's existence reconceived in the 1960s as a preparation for another Shoah, continuous aggression seemed the only feasible solution to the Palestinian question. Bellicosity came to be perceived as necessary, not only to quell Palestinian claims on Israeli territory, but also to avenge the powerlessness of European Jews during the Shoah and wash off the shame of their passive victimhood. The Shoah thus became the sacred core of Israeli nationalism; and it rendered political negotiation meaningless, while serving to justify the grossest forms of violence and dispossession as self-defence.

The sanctification of the Shoah and Israeli power has made the most well-intentioned forms of 'liberal' Zionism seem a cynical deception, one more way of buying time for a non-existent 'peace process' while claiming the intellectual prestige and moral superiority of liberalism. There was also, in many eyes, another 'terrible price' paid by a 'glorious Jewish tradition', as the Israeli-Palestinian writer Emile Habibi lamented in the mid-1980s. 'I cannot imagine,' he wrote, 'that, had the Holocaust not happened, the brothers of Heinrich

Heine and Maimonides, Bertolt Brecht and Stefan Zweig, Albert Einstein and the immortal Arab-Jewish poet Shlomo Ben Ovadia would have permitted a Jewish government to expel another Semite people out of its home.'

The Italian Jewish poet and critic Franco Fortini similarly grieved in 1989, claiming that Israel acted 'as France acted in Algeria, the United States in Vietnam or the Soviet Union in Hungary or Afghanistan'. Fortini was pained by Israel's decay because 'the Jews, long before Sharon's soldiers, were the bearers of a part of our sacred vessels, an anguished and ardent part of our words and wills'. There is a risk in such dirges of singling out Jews as exceptional, whether as consummate cosmopolitans and modernists or fanatical ethnonationalists. Nevertheless, as the soldiers of Israel take selfies against a backdrop of burning libraries and dynamited universities in Gaza, loss is a pervasive feeling today among both Jews and those who regard the Jewish experience of modernity as a touchstone for art, thought and morality.

And yet there are more unbearable ironies in Israel's moral cul-de-sac. In the first half of the twentieth century, demagogues claiming to represent historic ethnonational communities blamed all movements towards global oneness, all attempts to break down barriers between countries, nations and languages such as capitalism, liberalism, democracy and socialism on Jews. The myth of a Jewish conspiracy to debilitate and subdue the world's ethnic nations was the basis of the Final Solution. In the first decades of the twenty-first century, Israel turned into a redoubt of vicious ethnonationalism, and a 'laboratory' for the production and testing of tools used by other ethnonationalists to repress their peoples.

Unable to present itself any longer as a pure victim, an object of other people's actions, the country reveals itself today as a highly unstable actor, implicating more than just Palestinians in its calamitous failure. As such, the first Jewish state is now of great and ominous significance not only to Jews worldwide; it forces others to define themselves in opposition to or agreement with it. Simply by existing, Israel holds up a mirror, impelling other peoples and societies to identify themselves and their moral consciousness. And the reflections reveal, in one society after another, that the incurable offence, as Primo Levi called it, continues to spread like an infection, and is an inexhaustible source of evil, eight decades after the Shoah.

Part Two

REMEMBERING TO
REMEMBER THE SHOAH

Germany from Antisemitism to Philosemitism

I have always looked upon virtue as the
stuff of which hypocrisy is made.

Balzac

There is no such thing as collective memory. All
memory is individual, unreproducible – it dies with
each person. What is called collective memory
is not a remembering but a stipulating that *this*
is important, and this is the story about how it
happened, with the pictures that lock the story
in our minds.

Susan Sontag

That Germany's Nazi regime had murdered millions of
Jews was widely known after 1945. It was also clear that,
as Saul Friedländer writes in *The Years of Extermination,
1939–1945* (2007), 'not one social group, not one religious
community, not one scholarly institution or professional association in Germany and throughout Europe
declared its solidarity with the Jews'. In fact, 'many

social constituencies, many power groups were directly involved in the expropriation of the Jews and eager, be it out of greed, for their wholesale disappearance'.

In *Neighbors* (2000), Jan T. Gross describes how on a single day in July 1941 Catholic inhabitants of the town of Jedwabne killed 1,600 of their Jewish neighbours. In *Golden Harvest* (2012), Gross cites an eyewitness to another mass killing of Polish Jews in the early weeks of Hitler's war on the Soviet Union: he found it 'difficult to name townspeople who did *not* plunder Jewish houses while their inhabitants were being incinerated in a large barn'. Later, the desire to profit from the Final Solution would make for an economic boom among villagers living around the death camps of Treblinka and Sobibor. When in France, as Jean Améry noted, 'survivors and refugees returned and laid claim to their former homes, simple housewives would occasionally state, with a peculiar mixture of satisfaction and annoyance, "Tiens, ils reviennent; on ne les a tout de même pas tous tué."'*

But for many years such stupefying events were not woven into a pattern. The term Holocaust itself entered into ordinary English usage only in the early 1960s; the Hebrew word 'Shoah' came even later into international parlance. In the 1940s and 50s, the Shoah was not seen as an atrocity separate from other atrocities of the war:

---

* 'Well, they're back; we didn't kill them all, did we?'

the attempted extermination of Slav populations, Gypsies, disabled people and gay people. During the trials of leading Nazis in Nuremberg, it took the French prosecutor François de Menthon more than an hour to even mention, in passing, the Nazi effort to exterminate European Jewry. The popular film made of the trial, *Judgment at Nuremberg* (1961), folded the mass murder of Jews into the larger category of the crimes of Nazism. William L. Shirer in his 1960 bestseller *The Rise and Fall of the Third Reich*, the first major introduction for millions to Nazism and the Second World War, devoted only a tiny fraction of his 1,200-page book to the murder of European Jewry. The English translation of Elie Wiesel's autobiographical novel *Night* (1960) suffered several rejections before finding a publisher, and initially sold very poorly.

Today, however, it appears that no historical atrocity in Europe has been so widely and comprehensively commemorated as the Shoah: it was partly how Jews became, Yuri Slezkine writes in *The Jewish Century*, 'the Chosen People of the postwar Western world' and Israel became its exceptional nation. It is a wholly unprecedented culture of remembrance, which has by now accumulated its own long history. This history shows that the collective memory of the Shoah in Europe as well as Israel did not merely spring organically from what transpired between 1939 and 1945; it was belatedly constructed, often very deliberately, and with specific political ends.

*

The Shoah did not play a large role in the collective memory of the war in the countries of Soviet-controlled Eastern and Central Europe. In their official version, Hitler was a fascist, anti-communist and extreme nationalist, and only secondarily an antisemite. Thus, history books and public commemorations in the Soviet Union, Poland, Czechoslovakia and East Germany emphasised the anti-fascist credentials of these countries' regimes, and played down, or even ignored, the Jewishness of the millions of victims. The extermination of the Jews receded even deeper into the background in places like Poland and Hungary when Soviet oppression followed the memory of German occupation.

In 1996, Switzerland, which had prided itself on its wartime neutrality, admitted its role in financing the Nazis in exchange for gold partly plundered from the bodies of Jews. In 2004 Poland acknowledged the victimisation of Polish Jews, and that same year the Romanian state acknowledged responsibility for the Holocaust. In 2012, Norway apologised for the role of Norwegian police in deporting Jews to Nazi concentration camps. In recent years, the French far-right leader Jean-Marie Le Pen, who notoriously described Nazi gas chambers to be 'a detail' in the history of the war, has been steadily disowned by his own daughter and political heir, Marine Le Pen, now a staunch supporter of Israel.

The acknowledgements came so late because, as Tony Judt argued in *Postwar* (2005), 'Holocaust recognition' became the 'entry ticket' to the European Union and its economic bonanza. Thus, countries with shameful histories of collaboration with the Nazis, such as Hungary, Poland, Romania, were suddenly eager to publicly commemorate the Holocaust, embrace a definition of antisemitism formulated by the Task Force for International Cooperation on Holocaust Education, Remembrance, and Research (now the International Holocaust Remembrance Alliance) that equates antisemitism with criticism of Israel, and observe the International Holocaust Remembrance Day on 27 January. The Jewish victims of Hitler went from being ignored to becoming the central reference point for the European Union's idea of a pan-European identity. Today, there is no more devoted European ally of Israel, and ruthless suppressor of pro-Palestinian protests, than Viktor Orbán, the despotic premier of Hungary, where hundreds of thousands of Jews were deported to death camps during the Second World War, and where Orbán's own party Fidesz has long partaken of a popular antisemitism.

Germany's own contrition and radical self-cleansing as the chief tormentor of European Jews ought to have been straightforward. No country, however, matches its convoluted journey from ground zero in 1945 to Gaza in 2023. In recent decades, solidarity with the Jewish state has burnished Germany's proud self-image as the only country that makes public remembrance of its criminal past the very foundation of its collective identity. Particularly since German reunification, a Shoah-centred memory has been comprehensively institutionalised. School curricula, which include trips to former concentration camps, and calendars emphasise anniversaries such as 27 January (the Soviet liberation of Auschwitz) and 8 May (the final surrender of the Nazis), and monuments, memorials and museums across the country commemorate the victims of German crimes. A resonant symbol of this memory culture is the Memorial to the Murdered Jews of Europe near the Brandenburg Gate in the national capital Berlin, probably the only major national monument to commemorate the victims of a nation rather than the nation itself.*

In 2008, then German chancellor Angela Merkel claimed before the Knesset that ensuring Israel's security was part of Germany's *Staatsräson*, or *raison d'état*. The phrase was repeatedly invoked, with more vehemence than clarity, by German leaders after 7 October 2023. Less than two months before the Hamas offensive, Israel had secured, with American blessing, its largest ever arms deal with Germany. German arms sales to Israel surged tenfold in 2023; the vast majority of sales were approved after 7 October, and fast-tracked

---

* The Holocaust Memorial faced much domestic resistance. Rudolf Augstein, the founder and editor of *Der Spiegel*, remarked in 1998 that it was designed to satisfy American 'East Coast' elites.

by German officials who insisted that permits for arms exports to Israel would receive special consideration. As Israel began to bomb homes, refugee camps, schools, hospitals, mosques and churches in Gaza, and Israeli cabinet ministers promoted their schemes for ethnic cleansing, the German chancellor Olaf Scholz reiterated the national orthodoxy: 'Israel is a country that is committed to human rights and international law and acts accordingly.' As Netanyahu's campaign of indiscriminate murder and destruction intensified, Ingo Gerhartz, the commander of the Luftwaffe, arrived in Tel Aviv hailing the 'accuracy' of Israeli pilots; he also had himself photographed, in uniform, donating blood for Israeli soldiers.

The German health minister Karl Lauterbach approvingly retweeted a video in which an English far-right agitator claims that the Nazis were more decent than Hamas. 'Watch and listen,' Karin Prien, a deputy chair of the Christian Democratic Union and education minister for Schleswig-Holstein, also retweeted. 'This is great,' Jan Fleischhauer, a former editor at *Der Spiegel*, wrote. 'Really great,' echoed Veronika Grimm, a member of the German Council of Economic Experts. In June 2024, as the number of Palestinians killed by Israel ran close to 40,000, women and children comprising more than two-thirds of the identified dead, Germany's Nobel laureate Herta Müller, whose father served with the Waffen-SS in Romania, was still comparing Hamas to the Nazis and accusing American students of endorsing antisemitic violence.

Die Welt claimed that 'Free Palestine is the new Heil Hitler' and *Die Zeit* alerted German readers to the evidently outrageous fact that 'Greta Thunberg openly sympathises with the Palestinians'. An open letter from Adam Tooze, Samuel Moyn, Amia Srinivasan and other distinguished scholars criticising a statement by Jürgen Habermas and others in defence of Israel's actions provoked an editor at the *Frankfurter Allgemeine Zeitung* to claim that Jews have an 'enemy' at universities in the form of post-colonial studies. When the minister of culture Claudia Roth was caught on camera applauding the Israeli film-maker Yuval Abraham and his Palestinian colleague Basel Adra at the Berlinale film festival, she clarified that her applause was intended only for 'the Jewish-Israeli' Abraham.

For months, German leaders put up the strongest resistance to joint European calls for a ceasefire. The German president of the European Commission Ursula von der Leyen unstintingly backed Israel's vengeful violence, much to the chagrin of her own colleagues, EU council president Charles Michel and the EU's foreign policy chief Josep Borrell; she also ignored repeated calls to sanction Israel from EU member countries such as Spain and Ireland. As late as May 2024, after severe rebukes of Israel from the International Criminal Court and the International Court of Justice, the German foreign minister Annalena Baerbock claimed to have witnessed a video of a Hamas militant raping an Israeli woman – no such video exists. In October 2024, as Israel bombed hospitals and tent encampments in Gaza, and blew up entire villages in Lebanon, she justified these violations of international law, asserting that civilians could lose their protected status in war. German authorities also launched a ruthless crackdown on public displays of support for Palestine. '[German] officials,' the *New York Times* reported in early December 2023, 'have been combing through social media posts and open letters, some going back over a decade.' State-funded cultural institutions have long penalised artists and intellectuals of non-Western ancestry who show any hint of sympathy for Palestinians, retracting awards and invitations; the German authorities have now turned to disciplining even Jewish writers, artists and activists. After 7 October, Candice Breitz, Deborah Feldman, Masha Gessen, Nancy Fraser joined those either cancelled or 'lectured', as Eyal Weizman put it, 'by the children and grandchildren of the perpetrators who murdered our families and who now dare to tell us that we are antisemitic'.

Visiting Germany after the war, Hannah Arendt confessed to being 'oppressed by a kind of pervasive public stupidity which cannot be trusted to judge correctly the most elementary events'. 'A great number of Germans,' she wrote, 'especially among the more educated, apparently are no longer capable of telling the truth even if they want to.' Witnessing the German public sphere in 2023 and 2024, it was hard to resist a similarly damning conclusion: that self-righteous hypocrisy had been normalised enough to turn into a mode of governance and thought. It was also hard not to think, as hypocrisy lapsed into self-deception, about Germany's past and fear for the political future of Europe's most important country.

'In less than six years,' Arendt marvelled, 'Germany laid waste the moral structure of Western society, committing crimes that nobody would have believed possible.' With the intimacy and bluntness of a former insider, she recorded that a 'general lack of emotion, at any rate this apparent heartlessness, sometimes covered over with cheap sentimentality, is only the most conspicuous outward symptom of a deep-rooted, stubborn, and at times vicious refusal to face and come to terms with what really happened'.

Such mentalities were partly manifest in German treatment of the Jewish displaced persons. They were still languishing in West Germany in 1952, when the Bavarian customs police launched a raid on a DP camp. The assault had, according to the *Manchester Guardian*, 'all the trade-marks of Nazi descents on the ghettoes of Berlin and Frankfurt in the past'. As the newspaper reported, quoting the camp committee, 'policemen yelled such slogans as "The crematoria are still there", "the gas chambers are waiting for you", and "This time you really will get it in the neck, you damned Jews"'. In Communist-run East Germany, antisemitism was more subtle, if not less lethal, closely mimicking Stalin's campaign against 'cosmopolitans', which assumed that most Jews were potential spies.

At the same time, as an American military officer told the photojournalist Margaret Bourke-White, many Germans were acting 'as though the Nazis were a strange race of Eskimos who came down from the North Pole and somehow invaded Germany'. Bourke-White herself remarked: 'I have yet to find a German who will admit to being a Nazi.' As late as 1949, Adorno wrote to Thomas Mann that aside from a 'couple of total and touching puppet-like villains', he hadn't met a Nazi yet, 'not simply in the ironic sense that people will not admit to having been Nazis, but in the far more disturbing sense that they believe they never were Nazis'. Not surprisingly, Mann decided, after visiting Germany that year, to settle in Zurich.

'Germany can only return to itself when we communicate with one another,' wrote the philosopher Karl Jaspers, who had remained in Germany throughout its Nazi paroxysm, risking death together with his Jewish wife. In a landmark series of lectures about German guilt delivered in the months after the end of the war, he urged:

Let us learn to talk to one another. That is, let us not merely repeat our opinion, but hear what the other person thinks. Let us not only assert, but reflect in context, listen for reasons, remain prepared to reach a new insight. Let us inwardly attempt to assume the position of the other. Yes, let us actually seek out that which contradicts us. Grasping what we hold in common within contradiction is more important than hastily fixing exclusive standpoints with which the conversation draws hopelessly to an end.

But the opportunity for such an open-ended public conversation based on individual reflection – as distinct from public accusations, denials, ritualised remembrance and ostentatious breast-beating – passed quickly. 'Insensibility,' the poet and critic Hans Magnus Enzensberger famously wrote, was the 'condition' of post-war West Germany's rapid success. In *Adenauer's Germany and the Nazi Past* (2002), Norbert Frei painstakingly measures the depth and the breadth in the early post-war years of popular German sentiment against prosecuting criminals of the Nazi era or ejecting tainted elites out of positions of power. Jaspers, who migrated to Switzerland in 1948, himself lost his confidence in German moral reconstruction, as the exigencies of the Cold War made the Federal Republic, aka West Germany, seem one of the bulwarks of the European resistance to Stalin.

As war broke out in Korea in June 1950, German industry and manpower began to appear crucial to the defence of the free world. It certainly seemed so to

Fritz ter Meer who had helped plan an Auschwitz satellite camp. Released in February 1951 from his Bavarian prison, he told the reporters gathered outside, 'Now that the Americans have Korea on their hands, they are a lot more friendly.'

In East Germany, surviving members of the Weimar-era German Communist Party, handpicked by Stalin, ejected former Nazi Party members from professional posts. The novelist Jurek Becker, who lived in both Germanys, pointed out that many Nazis in Soviet-controlled East Germany moved to the West in order to feel safer under American occupation. The British historian Mary Fulbrook confirms in *Reckonings* (2018) that 'former Nazis in East Germany had roughly six or seven times the chance of being prosecuted and found guilty than they would have had if living in the West'.* As for West Germany, Fulbrook calculates that of the nearly million people who 'were at one point or another actively involved in killing Jewish civilians' (the number of enablers was much higher), 'only 6,656 were convicted of Nazi crimes' – 'fewer even than the number of people who had been employed at Auschwitz alone'. By the end of the twentieth century, only 164 individuals had been sentenced for the crime of murder – of six million Jews. In *Into That Darkness* Gitta Sereny recalls meeting, at his

---

* In the 1950s and 60s, East Germany secured many propaganda victories out of West Germany's amnesty to Nazis.

idyllic Bavarian home, the man who in Treblinka used to stand with a whip at the door to the gas chambers and drive Jews in.

In a March 2024 article for *Dissent*, historian Hans Kundnani wrote,

> by the mid-1950s, the elite in the civil service, judiciary, and academia had largely reverted to that of the Third Reich. Many young people growing up in West Germany felt they were 'surrounded by Nazis', as one person I interviewed put it. By the mid-1960s, they had begun to see not just personal continuities but structural ones: the Federal Republic was a fascist, or at least 'pre-fascist', state. The student movement emerged as a protest against these real and imagined continuities.

Indeed, a powerful myth emphasised German suffering after the war; it stressed that Germany was a nation of victims, particularly POWs in Soviet hands and those expelled from Eastern and Central Europe. Robert G. Moeller describes in *War Stories* (2001) how rising anti-communism in Germany drew conveniently on Nazi stereotypes of the Russian 'Mongol' who had raped and pillaged his way to Berlin. In 1946, Konrad Adenauer, later the chancellor of West Germany, wrote to a friend who had immigrated to the United States that since 'Asia stands at the Elbe', 'the danger is great' and only a strong Europe with American help can 'stop the further spiritual and forceful advance of Asia'. In a later variation on this theme of a civilised West menaced by hordes from the East, the conservative German historian Ernst Nolte would claim that the Nazis came to commit 'Asiatic' deeds because of their justified fear of otherwise falling victim to them.

When in March 1960 Adenauer met his Israeli counterpart, David Ben-Gurion, in New York, he had not only been presiding over a systematic reversal of the de-Nazification process decreed by the country's Western occupiers in 1945, he had also been aiding the suppression of the unprecedented horror of the Judaeocide. The German people, according to Adenauer, were also victims of Hitler. What's more, he went on, most Germans under Nazi rule had 'joyfully helped fellow Jewish citizens whenever they could'.

In September 1952 Adenauer had agreed to a deal that would compensate the State of Israel to the extent of some 3.45 billion Deutsche Marks. The deal was not popular: in 1951, only 5 per cent of Germans had admitted to guilt over the fate of the Jews, and 21 per cent thought that 'the Jews themselves were partly responsible for what happened to them during the Third Reich'. More embarrassingly, some in Adenauer's own party voted against the deal. Nevertheless, Adenauer's language at his meeting with Ben-Gurion was unambiguous: Israel, he said, is a 'fortress of the West' and 'I can already now tell you that we will help you, we will not leave you alone'.

West Germany's munificence towards Israel had motivations beyond national shame or duty, or the personal beliefs and prejudices of a chancellor who as vice president of the German Colonial Society had urged the German Reich to possess colonies in order to create more living space for the German people, and who loathed the Arab nationalism of Gamal Abdel Nasser (referring to him as 'little Hitler' during the Anglo-French-Israeli assault on Egypt in 1956). As the Cold War intensified, Adenauer determined that his country needed greater sovereignty and a more significant role in Western economic and security alliances; Germany's 'long road west' (the title of historian Heinrich Winkler's bestselling book about German history) lay through Israel.

West Germany moved quickly along that road after 1960, becoming the most important supplier of military hardware to Israel in addition to being the main enabler of its economic modernisation. Adenauer himself explained after his retirement that giving money and weapons to Israel was essential to restoring Germany's 'international standing', adding that 'the power of the Jews even today, especially in America, should not be underestimated'.

Franz Josef Strauss, a veteran of the Wehrmacht in the

*

bloodlands of Eastern Europe who became Adenauer's defence minister and later premier of Bavaria, thought that *Vergangenheitsbewältigung*, or coming to terms with the past, was best accomplished by defence deals with Israel (which he pursued secretly with Shimon Peres in the late 1950s). Rolf Vogel, a journalist and fixer for Adenauer, who claimed that 'the Uzi in the hand of the German soldier is better than any brochure against anti-semitism', now seems an early exponent of this mode of dealing with the past.

The post-war German–Israeli symbiosis was at the centre of the 'unprincipled political gamesmanship', in Primo Levi's bitter words, that expedited the reha-bilitation of Germany only a few years after the full extent of its genocidal antisemitism became known. By the mid-1960s, when Jean Améry travelled through Germany, the country was savouring its so-called eco-nomic miracle, partly due to the American loans that were also sparking a broader European recovery. In 'the industrial paradise of the New Europe', Améry found himself unexpectedly discussing the latest Euro-pean and American novels with Germany's 'refined' intellectuals.

Yet the survivor of Auschwitz could not expunge from his memory the 'stony faces' of Germans before a pile of corpses at a railway platform or of the Flem-ish SS man who beat him on the head with a shovel handle whenever he didn't work fast enough. And he would discover, 'to my own distress', that in this 'thriving land', he bore a new 'grudge' against Germans and their exalted place in the 'majestic halls of the West'.

The flip side of West Germany's accommodation of Nazis was what Améry called an 'obtrusive philosemitism'. This philosemitism, parasitic on old antisemitic stereotypes, and combined with sentimental images of Jews, still shapes Germany's relationship to Israel, and is now even more obtrusive. By 1965, Eleonore Sterling, a survivor of the Shoah and Germany's first female professor of political science, was describing how 'a functional philosemitic attitude' had replaced 'a true act of understanding, repentance and future vigilance'. Peter Gay recalls in his memoir *My German Question* (1998) that 'there were some fifteen thousand Jews in the country in 1945 compared with half a million in 1933, and gentile Germans treated them with a kind of greasy delicacy, an ostentatious admiration for everything that Jews said, did, or believed'.

Gay, who had fled Nazi Germany with his Jewish family in 1939 to Cuba, was among the German Jews 'sickened' by this 'newfound love'. So was the novelist Manès Sperber. 'Your philosemitism depresses me,' he wrote to a colleague, 'degrades me like a compliment that is based on an absurd misunderstanding . . . You overestimate us Jews in a dangerous fashion and insist on loving our entire people. I don't request this, I do not wish for us – or any other people – to be loved in this way.' But the philosemitism was also a strategic mode of self-regard. Arendt, writing to Karl Jaspers from Jerusalem in April 1961, reported that the Germans present at the trial of Adolf Eichmann were 'displaying an unpleasant overeagerness and finding absolutely everything wonderful. Enough to make you throw up, if I may say so. One of them has already flung his arms around my neck and burst into tears.'

In his pages on the trial of Eichmann in *Germany and Israel* (2020), Daniel Marwecki describes how visions of Israel as a new embodiment of Jewish power also awakened not so long dormant German fantasies. A report by the West German delegation to the Eichmann trial marvelled at 'the novel and very advantageous type of the Israeli youth', who are 'of great height, often blond and blue-eyed, free and self-determined in their movements with well-defined faces' and exhibit 'almost none of the features which one used to view as Jewish'. On 7 June 1967, the *Frankfurter Allgemeine Zeitung* greeted Israel's victory with an editorial titled 'Der Blitzkrieg Israels'; the phrase associated with the Nazi assault on Europe was then emblazoned on the front pages of *Die Zeit* and *Der Spiegel* (which commented on German blood donations for Israel with 'Aryan blood flowed for the Jews'). *Die Welt* regretted German 'infamies' about the Jewish people: the belief that they were 'without national sentiment; never ready for battle, but always keen to profit from somebody else's war effort'. The Jews were in fact a 'small, brave, heroic, genius people'.

Axel Springer, whose eponymous company published *Die Welt*, and who was among the major post-war employers of superannuated Nazis, boasted after the Six Day War that he had published Israeli newspapers in Germany for six days.* The German New Left that turned anti-Israel around this time, alienating Jean Améry among others, was partly reacting to Springer's truculent propaganda, as well as to the presence of Nazis in the civil service, judiciary and academia, and the murder, on 2 June 1967, three days before the Six Day War, by the West Berlin police of a student at a demonstration against the Shah of Iran's visit to the city.

Hospitality for the US-backed Iranian despot was probably the least unsavoury aspect of West German foreign policy towards decolonising Asia and Africa in the 1960s. West Germany supported France's attempt to kill and torture Algerian rebels into submission; it stood by Belgium as it undertook rearguard action against a liberation

---

* The suspicion that a now taboo nationalism is projected onto a proxy state is deepened by Mathias Döpfner, present-day CEO of Axel Springer, whose self-declared motto is 'Zionismus über alles' (Zionism above all). The phrase alludes to the erstwhile first line of the German national anthem, 'Deutschland Über Alles', which was deleted due to its association with Nazi Germany.

movement in Congo. Moïse Tshombe, the puppet of Belgian mining interests, who was responsible for the murder of Patrice Lumumba, enjoyed state hospitality in Bonn in 1964. West Germany was the main supplier of arms to Portugal in its desperate struggles against anti-colonialists in Africa; and apartheid in South Africa found a stalwart defender in Gustav Adolf Sonnenhol, a former SS officer sent to South Africa as Bonn's ambassador in 1968. Not surprisingly, East Germany advertised its break with the Third Reich's racial politics by ostentatiously denouncing West Germany's support for South Africa, and championing the African National Congress (ANC).

In *Foreign Front* (2012), Quinn Slobodian adds more political context to the New Left that troubled Améry, particularly the three years (1966–9) when Kurt Georg Kiesinger, a former Nazi, was German chancellor. It was, he writes, 'the vocal support of West German political parties across the spectrum for the U.S. military intervention in Vietnam' that 'helped catalyze leftist opposition'. West Germany was trying to appease the US government, which had suggested the deployment of West German troops to Vietnam: 'The defense of Berlin,' Defense Secretary Robert McNamara said in 1964, 'starts at the Mekong.' West Germany settled for being the second largest provider of civilian aid to the puppet South Vietnam regime maintained by the United States.

Many students, including future terrorists such as Ulrike Meinhof, had idealised the United States as a defender of freedom and democracy; they became disturbed by reports of American carpet bombing of Vietnam, using napalm designed to remove skin, and bombs built to explode in mid-air and inject shrapnel into flesh. They were frustrated, too, by the malicious caricatures of their idealism by Springer's tabloid press as well as the German political establishment. 'Fighting for the defense of Western freedom with carpet bombing,' according to an activist quoted by Slobodian, did not only injure the 'moral feelings' of many young Germans: 'The entire existing framework for understanding the world was put into question.'

Figuring Jewish Israelis as Aryan warriors, the German press further undermined that framework for understanding the world. At any rate, *Bild* likening Moshe Dayan to Erwin Rommel wasn't a contradiction. Such comparisons were an imperative for some beneficiaries of the German economic miracle. Marwecki writes that Adenauer made a major loan and the supply of military equipment 'dependent on the Israeli handling of the trial' of Adolf Eichmann: he had been shocked to learn of Mossad's discovery of Eichmann just weeks after his meeting with Ben-Gurion (he didn't know that a German Jewish prosecutor had secretly informed the Israelis about Eichmann's whereabouts) and feared what Eichmann might reveal.

He went to extraordinary lengths to ensure that his closest confidant, Hans Globke, wasn't fingered as an exponent of Nuremberg racial laws at the trial. The potential for embarrassment was great: Globke, under investigation by federal officials for his role in the deportation of Greek and Slovak Jews, was the main intermediary between Adenauer and the Israeli foreign ministry. Many other sordid details remain locked up in the classified files of the German Chancellery and German intelligence. The philosopher Bettina Stangneth found enough in the archives to show, in *Eichmann Before Jerusalem* (2014), that Adenauer enlisted the CIA to delete a reference to Globke from an article in *Life* magazine. It is also now known that, acting on Adenauer's instructions, Rolf Vogel stole potentially incriminating files on Globke from an East German lawyer at the King David Hotel in Jerusalem. As it turned out, much to Adenauer's relief, his new Israeli allies protected Globke.

Yeshayahu Leibowitz remarked many years after Eichmann was hanged that his 'trial was a total failure; Eichmann really was a small and insignificant cog in a big machine. I think it was a conspiracy by Adenauer and Ben-Gurion to clear the name of the German people. In exchange they paid us billions.' Marwecki provides the belated evidence for this scandalous claim while describing the 'exchange structure specific to German-Israeli relations': moral absolution of an insufficiently de-Nazified and still profoundly antisemitic Germany in return for cash and weapons.

The deal also had other 'political aims and very important political consequences', as the Israeli writer Boaz

Evron pointed out in 1981. It strengthened 'German guilt consciousness for the Germans themselves, and more importantly, in the eyes of the world surrounding them', thus forcing Germany 'to act against its own interests and to apply to Israel a special preferential relationship, without Israel seeing itself obligated to reciprocate'.

Damagingly for Israel, 'the system of relations with Germany' became 'a blueprint for relations between Israel and most of the states of the Christian West, first and foremost the United States'.

Cheap discharge of guilt was one motivation. Back in the early 1960s, however, it greatly suited Germany as well as Israel to portray Arab adversaries of Israel, including Nasser (dubbed 'Hitler on the Nile' by the *Daily Mail*), as the true embodiments of Nazism. The Eichmann trial underplayed the persistence of Nazi support in Germany while exaggerating the Nazi presence in Arab countries. As Arendt exasperatedly wrote, Globke 'had more right than the ex-Mufti of Jerusalem to figure in the history of what the Jews had actually suffered from the Nazis'. She noted, too, that Ben-Gurion, while reaffirming some Germans as 'decent', made no 'mention of decent Arabs'.

In *Subcontractors of Guilt* (2023), Esra Özyürek describes the way that German politicians, officials and journalists, now that the far right is in the ascendant, crank up the old mechanism of sanitising Germany by demonising Muslims. The neo-Nazi Alternative für Deutschland, whose co-chairman Alexander Gauland argued that 'if the French are rightly proud of their emperor and the Britons of Nelson and Churchill, we have the right to be proud of the achievements of the German soldiers in two world wars', has become the country's second most popular party. In September 2024, it became the first far-right party since the Second World War to have the largest number of seats in one of Germany's sixteen state parliaments. Yet despite the undisguised antisemitism of even mainstream politicians such as Hubert Aiwanger, the deputy minister president of Bavaria, 'white Christian-background Germans' see themselves 'as having reached their destination of redemption and re-democratisation', according to Özyürek.

The 'general German social problem of antisemitism' is projected onto a minority of Middle Eastern immigrants, who are then further stigmatised as 'the most unrepentant antisemites' in need of 'additional education and disciplining'. To denounce Germany's Muslim minority as 'the major carriers of antisemitism', as Özyürek points out, is to suppress the fact that nearly '90 per cent of antisemitic crimes are committed by right-wing white Germans'. This was verified soon after 7 October, when both Judaeophobia and Islamophobia increased in Germany. The German president, Frank-Walter Steinmeier, urged all those in Germany with 'Arab roots' to disavow hatred of Jews and denounce Hamas. The vice chancellor, Robert Habeck, issued a more explicit warning to Muslims: they would be tolerated in Germany only if they rejected anti-semitism. Aiwanger, a politician with a weakness for Nazi salutes, joined the chorus, blaming antisemitism in Germany on 'unchecked immigration'. 'In contemporary Germany,' a 2023 article in *Jewish Currents* pointed out, 'a questionably conceived anti-antisemitism has become the mechanism for keeping Germanness Aryan.'

In *Never Again* (2023), Andrew I. Port suggests that the conviction among Germans that 'they had left the rabid racism of their forebears far behind them may have paradoxically allowed for the unabashed expression of different forms of racism'. This partly accounts for the extraordinary callousness, bordering on racial contempt, in Germany over the fate of Palestinians. Increasingly, Germany's much-lauded culture of historical memory seems to have maintained an appearance of success only because the German ruling class had, until recently, less occasion to expose its historical delusions than, for instance, the Brexiteers dreaming of imperial-era strength and self-sufficiency.

It is almost as though by claiming to embody the Shoah's most hectic memory culture Germany managed to avoid reckoning with the crimes that necessitated that culture in the first place. In 1975, the literary critic Hans Mayer, who moved from East to West Germany in 1963, derided 'the fundamentally unsound relationship of the average German toward the phenomenon of the Jew and the state of Israel'. This unsoundness is now manifest in a variety of ways, including in the number of Germans fraudulently claiming to be Jewish, as a May 2024 article in *The Baffler* detailed in harrowing fashion.

According to the philosopher Susan Neiman, 'German historical reckoning has gone haywire'. Neiman, who wrote admiringly of *Vergangenheitsbewältigung* in *Learning from the Germans* (2019), now believes that Germany's 'philosemitic fury' has been turned against Jews in Germany. But then, as the historian Frank Stern unsparingly diagnosed in *The Whitewashing of the Yellow Badge* (1992), German philosemitism is primarily a 'political instrument', used not only to 'justify options in foreign policy', but also 'to evoke and project a moral stance in times when domestic tranquillity is threatened by antisemitic, anti-democratic and right-wing extremist phenomena'.* Thus, German Israel-philia and philosemitism is peaking just as there is again a recrudescence in Germany of far-right furies.

This perverse dialectic explains why Germany ignores, while endlessly commemorating the Shoah and proclaiming its undying support for Israel, the atrocities Germans inflicted on Asians and Africans even during the brief rampages of German colonialism. In

---

* In *Germans and Jews Since the Holocaust* (2015), Pól Ó Dochartaigh cites a study after German reunification showing that East Germans, though officially hostile to Israel, were less antisemitic than their counterparts in the West. Certainly, Jewish writers such as Jurek Becker, Anna Seghers, Peter Edel, Victor Klemperer, Hans Mayer and Arnold Zweig found East Germany a more congenial place for Jews after the war.

China in 1900–1, committed to crushing the 'Yellow Peril', German troops faithfully followed their Kaiser's instructions to behave like 'Huns'. Then in 1904 in German South-West Africa (contemporary Namibia) the German imperial army – led by Lothar von Trotha, who had helped quell the Boxer Rebellion in China a few years before – killed an estimated 65,000 Herero people out of a total population of approximately 80,000. It is a genocide that Germany has failed fully to acknowledge, let alone pay adequate reparations for, despite repeated demands from the government of Namibia. German colonialists suppressing another uprising in East Africa in 1905–7 executed, with machine guns, dozens of people at a time – altogether 80,000 people died in the fighting and another 200,000 were consumed in the famine that followed.*

Many more Africans, 350,000 in one estimate, were killed between 1914 and 1918, when Germany, attempting to hold on to its colonies, turned the natives under its control into grist for the First World War's slaughter machine. Edward Paice claims in *Tip and Run* (2007) that 'German participants in the campaign experienced no "war guilt" whatsoever' and their hundreds of

---

* Readers in Germany vicariously participated in this colonial violence through the novel by Gustav Frenssen, *Peter Moor's Journey to Southwest Africa* (1906). A bestseller in Germany, it was reprinted by the Nazis in special editions for schools and the Wehrmacht.

thousands of African victims were 'erased from German history'. The Nobel laureate Abdulrazak Gurnah, whose grandfather in Zanzibar was conscripted as a carrier by German troops, is among many who have wondered 'why the history and experience of German colonialism in Africa was so ferociously brutal'. But then Germany (and Italy), which came later than its European peers to an exploitable Asia and Africa, was particularly desperate to divert outwards, towards hapless natives, the great internal tensions built up over decades of uneven social and economic modernisation.

Allied powers forced premature decolonisation upon a defeated Germany at Versailles. But loss of colonised lands, followed by occupation of German territory by black French soldiers, only built up large reservoirs of violent passions. Raffael Scheck describes in *Hitler's African Victims* (2006) how the killing sprees of the *Einsatzgruppen* in the East – shooting people by the edge of mass graves which the victims themselves had been forced to dig – were prefigured by the massacres in May and June 1940 of thousands of French African soldiers.

It is another barely acknowledged crime of German aggrandisement. But there are no incentives to project a moral stance in the case of black Africans, let alone declare their well-being to be Germany's *Staatsräson* as domestic tranquillity is again threatened by antisemitic,

anti-democratic and right-wing extremist phenomena.*
The political and moral deformations and intellectual
helplessness of Germany today are more dangerous
than at any other time since 1945. A senior leader of
the Alternative für Deutschland – and now their lone
member in the European Parliament – asserted in May
2024 that not all members of the SS had been criminals. The party's leader in Thuringia, Björn Höcke, was
fined twice in 2024 for using banned Nazi slogans in his
speeches. German courts are currently trying a far-right
group for plotting the violent overthrow of the government. In 2024, on the seventy-fifth anniversary of
its Basic Law – the constitutional document which in
1949 carefully set out the country's liberal democracy –
Germany looks feeble again before the economic crises
and social breakdowns of capitalism that first produced
fascism.

Responding to Nolte's description of barbarism as
uniquely 'Asiatic', Germany's pre-eminent philosopher
Jürgen Habermas had hailed the 'unconditional opening

---

* The genocide scholar Dirk Moses diagnosed these pathologies of
denial in his much-discussed 2021 essay on the 'German catechism'. 'The
sacrifice of Jews in the Holocaust by Nazis,' he wrote 'is the premise
for the Federal Republic's legitimacy.' Therefore, 'the Holocaust is more
than an important historical event. It is a sacred trauma that cannot be
contaminated by profane ones – meaning non-Jewish victims and other
genocides – that would vitiate its sacrificial function.'

of the Federal Republic to the political culture of the West' as the most important achievement of post-war Germany. The intellectual justification for taking the road to the West after the war was that Germans had strayed too far off it, and ended up committing monstrous crimes. Thus Habermas, a former member of the Hitler Youth, hailed an exemplary 'Western civilization' from which Germans had unwisely dissociated themselves. Germans could become part of a superior West again by putting the Shoah and undying commitment to Israel at the centre of their collective identity and by renouncing ethnonationalism.

But this entire existing framework for understanding the world, and Germany's place in it, has been tottering in recent years. Habermas and others have convinced themselves their country safely converted to liberalism on its high road to the West through Israel; they don't, however, seem to ponder the fact that the old idea of the West has never seemed more incoherent and unconvincing. Refined during the Cold War, it had a large, self-flattering Anglo-American component, signifying, in opposition to totalitarian regimes, electoral democracy, free markets and individual freedoms. But the United States has lurched in the last decade from calamitously failed wars to far-right demagoguery, and Britain, deceived by blustery rogues into Brexit, is unlikely to recover soon from an extreme act of self-harm. The 'political culture of the West', from which Hitler borrowed his racial conception of citizenship, does not inspire great admiration even within the West today. Revealingly, the binary of the enlightened West and unenlightened East, once used to authorise the Nazi quest for *Lebensraum* in the East and then adapted to serve Cold War policy agendas, is the currency today of far-right nationalists across Israel, Europe and America. During Israel's assault on Gaza, Netanyahu announced that he is fighting the 'new Nazis' in Gaza in order to save 'Western civilisation', while others in his cohort of Jewish supremacists kept up a supporting chorus denouncing the people of Gaza as 'subhuman', 'animals' and 'Nazis'. Hitler himself was convinced, when Jews were conceived as subhuman and animals, that the fate of Western civilisation rested on his shoulders, his capacity to destroy the enemy within. And there was much about Western democracies, especially their foundations in white supremacy, and cultures of racism and antisemitism, that allowed Hitler to believe that they would welcome his extermination of Jews.

Germany's post-war quest for normalisation, whether through philosemitism and West-philia, or *Staatsräson* and proud and ostentatious self-reproach, has reached, perhaps too predictably, a dead end. It always seemed implausible that a collective moral education could produce a stable, homogeneous attitude across the generations. There are too many other factors determining what is remembered and what is forgotten, and the German national subconscious is burdened by a century of secrecy, crimes and cover-ups. It should not surprise us then that, as *völkisch*-authoritarian racism surged at home, Germany yet again became complicit, through its unconditional solidarity with Netanyahu, Smotrich, Gallant and Ben-Gvir, in murderous ethnonationalism. As Günter Grass wrote in *Crabwalk* (2002), 'History, or, to be more precise, the history we Germans have repeatedly mucked up, is a clogged toilet. We flush and flush, but the shit keeps rising.'

Americanising the Holocaust

Some people remember where they were the day
President John F. Kennedy was shot. Others
remember where they were when the space shuttle
Challenger went down. I remember where I was the
day I discovered Israel.

Thomas Friedman

The meaning and message of the Shoah were always
prone to redefinition; they were accordingly made and
disbursed in different ways to serve some perceived
needs of the present. Nor were the ideological manip-
ulations of the memory of the Shoah politically and
morally benign. The struggle of memory against forgetting in this instance was no simple struggle of people
against authoritarian power. In almost every Western
country, the obligation to remember and commemorate the Shoah suppressed, often deliberately, much
awkward history, broadening the scope for authoritarian politics.

In the free world, a full reckoning with Jewish agony
was initially postponed by some shameful facts. Contrary to popular myths about the Second World War,

Allied powers hadn't fought to liberate Jews from their persecutors, or to uphold the values of democracy in its existential battle against totalitarianism. The Nazi war on the Jews, which built up through the 1930s before reaching its apogee in the Final Solution, created hundreds of thousands of Jewish refugees. But neither the American State Department nor the British Foreign Office wished to rescue them. On the contrary: they consistently feared, and worked to avoid, a situation in which Germany and its allies would force out tens of thousands of Jews into Allied hands.

Neville Chamberlain, who wrote in a letter to his sister after Kristallnacht that 'no doubt Jews aren't a lovable people; I don't care about them myself, but that is not sufficient to explain the pogrom', made a semi-compassionate exception when he pushed for the Kindertransport scheme which brought almost 10,000 unaccompanied Jewish children to Britain on the eve of war in 1939. Yet British policy aimed at obstructing rescue possibilities and creating public opinion against Jewish refugees. An article in the *Observer* in 1938 typically posed the question, 'If a further accretion of, say, 100,000 [Jewish refugees] come into the country, how could the danger be averted of an anti-Jewish feeling here?' In 1945, the Labour home secretary argued for the return of Jewish refugees to Germany on the basis that there was less antisemitism there.

*

Nor were the British more inclined to house Jewish refugees in their vast empire, including the place that they had promised to Jews during the previous world war as their 'national home'. The historian Bernard Wasserstein, whose own mother was detained in Palestine, records in *Britain and the Jews of Europe, 1939–45* (1979) how on the second day of the war in 1939, British soldiers fired on Jewish refugees, including women and children, on an overpeopled hulk as they attempted to land on Tel Aviv beach. Recent efforts by British governments to 'stop the boats' and send asylum seekers to Africa are hardly innovative. In late 1940, British authorities in Palestine deported 1,580 Jews, nearly half of them women and children, to Mauritius, where the survivors of a typhus epidemic on board their ship were interned in a camp surrounded by barbed wire and guards.

That same year, tens of thousands of Jewish refugees were interned on the British Isles, notably on the Isle of Man, amid general panic about enemy agents and fifth columnists.* In one of the more notorious episodes of this mass internment, obscure compared to the American corralling of over 100,000 persons of Japanese origin in 1942, police entered Hampstead Public Library

* *The Holocaust Encyclopedia* (2001) notes that 'in Britain the administrators and the police in the Channel Islands . . . who had helped with the deportation of Jews continued to work in their old positions, and some of them even received the Order of the British Empire for the bravery they had shown in the war years'.

and arrested all people there of German and Austrian descent.

By November 1942, British and American authorities could no longer publicly deny the shocking information trickling out of Europe: that the Nazis were systematically exterminating European Jewry. Still official policy did not soften. On 17 December 1942 in the House of Commons, the foreign secretary Anthony Eden sonorously read out an Allied declaration condemning Nazi persecution of the Jews and promising punishment for the perpetrators. Later that same month Eden and his colleagues decided at a Cabinet meeting that Britain could not admit more than two thousand refugees.

Barriers to Jewish refugee emigration were higher in the United States. In a country that claimed to be perennially open to newcomers, a myth burnished by the Statue of Liberty installed in New York Harbor in 1886, organised antisemitic, xenophobic and racist groups wielded enormous political power; they managed to, first, exclude Asian immigrants through restrictive laws in 1882 and 1917, and then drastically limit Jewish immigration in 1924. Too many Jews 'create chaos', the celebrity aviator Charles Lindbergh noted in his journal while sailing to New York from Europe in April 1939. And, he added, voicing a common sentiment in American society, 'there are too many in places like New York already'.

In 1938, Rafael Trujillo, the infamous dictator of the Dominican Republic, offered to accept up to 100,000

Jewish refugees in an eccentric attempt to 'whiten' his citizenry. After the initial settlement of a few hundred Jews, however, the American denial of transit visas turned his project into a non-starter. When in May 1939 more than nine hundred refugees, mostly Jewish, sailed from Hamburg to Havana on the *St. Louis*, only to find that their visas had been annulled by the Cuban government (the Cuban visa officer had taken bribes), the US State Department refused them entry, saying that they would have to wait their turn in Europe for US visas. After Jewish organisations stepped in as sponsors, England, Belgium, France and the Netherlands agreed to accept some of the refugees on their return to Europe in 1939. More than 250, including many admitted to France and the Netherlands, still died at the hands of the Nazis.

White supremacists in the State Department ensured, as David S. Wyman records in *The Abandonment of the Jews* (1984), that 'only 21,000 refugees were allowed to enter the United States during the three and one-half years the nation was at war with Germany . . . 10 percent of the number who could have been legally admitted under the immigration quotas during that period'.

'I am forced to look out for emigration and as far as I can see USA is the only country we could go to,' Otto Frank wrote from Amsterdam to an American friend on 30 April 1941. The recipient of the letter and potential rescuer of Anne Frank, Otto's daughter, was a friend of the US president and his wife, Eleanor. Yet even he could not overcome the US immigration restrictions, which, greatly esteemed by Hitler, were actually further strengthened during the war, finally resulting in the exclusion of hundreds of thousands of Jews who could have avoided murder by the Nazis.*

More Jewish refugees from Nazism were able to leave Europe in the final year of the war. The British government responded by seeking to prevent their departure, interdicting refugees on high seas and interning them. Fewer immigrants than those permitted under its own White Paper in 1939, which abrogated the Balfour Declaration and limited Jewish immigration to 75,000 for five years, managed to reach Palestine. And from 1946 onwards, Cyprus, then a British colony, held more than 50,000 Jews, mainly survivors of the Shoah from Europe, in camps. The British refused to allow men of military age to leave these camps even after May 1948, when the newly established State of Israel opened its doors to all Jewish newcomers. The camps were not dismantled until early 1949.

Reports during wartime about the maltreatment of Jews were sparse and tentatively received, and often

---

* There were a few exceptions, notably Varian Fry, and Hiram Bingham, a diplomat at the US consulate in Marseille in the late 1930s. He managed to pull off the escape from Europe of, among others, Marc Chagall, André Breton, Lion Feuchtwanger, Alma Mahler, Franz Werfel, Heinrich Mann and a then unknown young thinker called Hannah Arendt, before he was stopped by superiors in the State Department and pushed to resign.

relegated to the inside pages in newspapers. Even after such reports became routine, they were met with widespread public doubts. A poll in January 1943 revealed disbelief among a majority of Americans that the Nazis could have exterminated two million Jews (the murders amounted to four million by then). Scepticism lingered even as the Soviet army began to liberate the death camps in Poland where most of the killings had taken place. As *Collier's* acknowledged in January 1945, 'a lot of Americans simply do not believe the stories of Nazi mass executions of Jews and anti-Nazi Gentiles in eastern Europe by means of gas chambers, freight cars partly loaded with lime and other horrifying devices. These stories are so foreign to most Americans' experience of life in this country that they seem incredible.'

Asserting their superior cultural and political power, Western powers later claimed, persuasively, to have been the main liberator of Jews from the Nazi camps. The images from Bergen-Belsen, which was freed by British troops, of mountains of corpses, cleared by bulldozers, became representative of the end of the Shoah. But the major centres of annihilation – Majdanek, Chelmno, Belzec, Sobibor, Treblinka and Auschwitz-Birkenau – were in the territory overrun by the Soviet army. Jews formed a minority among the inmates of the camps liberated by Allied troops. Nor was liberation the exuberant event it was later presented in films such as *Life Is Beautiful* (1997) and *Schindler's List* (1993), and documentaries, museum displays and books. For the survivors, 'the hour of freedom struck solemn and oppressive', Primo Levi wrote. As for the liberators,

> They didn't greet us, they didn't smile; they appeared oppressed, not only by pity but by a confused restraint, which sealed their mouths, and riveted their eyes to the mournful scene. It was a shame well-known to us, the shame that inundated us after the selections and every time we had to witness or submit to an outrage: the shame that the Germans didn't know, and which the just man feels before a sin committed by another.

The survivors still had to endure many shocks and tribulations, many of them unexpectedly from their liberators. In 1946 in the Polish town of Kielce, 180 kilometres south of Warsaw, a mob of antisemites killed forty of the two hundred Jews who had survived the mass murder of the town's 25,000 Jewish inhabitants. Two of the Polish survivors rescued by Oskar Schindler were murdered on their return to their home town. Many other Jews returned to their places of origin only to discover they could no longer call those places home. One result was that from Eastern Europe more than 100,000 Jewish refugees fled to Germany – the original source of their torment. Munich, the capital of Nazism, became their temporary refuge, the place where they could feel safe before moving on to America or Palestine. Little did they know another kind of ordeal was just beginning.

David Nasaw, in *The Last Million* (2020), is one of the recent historians to describe how 250,000 Jews were condemned to a state of limbo for years in displaced persons camps run by the Allies as no country was initially willing to accept them. America's immigration laws continued to prevent the entry of a large number of East European Jews long after the war. The British permitted the entry of more than 200,000 Eastern Europeans, and 15,000 German and 8,000 Ukrainian POWs, while asserting that large-scale immigration 'could only be welcomed without reserve if the immigrants were of good human stock' – a category that excluded Jewish DPs as well as black immigrants from the British Commonwealth.

At the same time, Britain, which had already limited Jewish immigration to Palestine in 1939, cracked down on survivors of the Shoah seeking refuge among their Jewish counterparts in the Promised Land. In *The Liberation of the Camps* (2015), Dan Stone describes British diplomats recycling Nazi stereotypes of 'Judeo-Bolshevism' in order to discourage Jewish emigration. 'Cynical exploitation of Holocaust survivors for Cold War gains,' Stone writes, 'continued throughout the postwar period.' The Soviet Union, for instance, sought to embarrass Western Allies by pointing to British moral failures and offering 'cynical, short-term support for Israeli independence'.

The US administration criticised British policy over Palestine, too, but with the calculation that Jewish emigration to Palestine would prevent Jews arriving in the US en masse. As it happened, about 200,000 of the Jewish survivors in Europe were forced to find refuge in Israel until 1953, when the US finally lowered, if only slightly, its barriers to entry and accepted some 80,000 of them. The camps in Cyprus, where tens of thousands of Jewish immigrants captured by the British were interned, replicated some of the humiliations of German camps. Nor were attitudes and conditions in American-occupied Germany any better. A report commissioned by US president Harry S. Truman after he heard reports of ill-treatment of Jews in American-occupied Bavaria said:

> As matters now stand, we appear to be treating the Jews as the Nazis treated them except that we do not exterminate them. They are in concentration camps in large numbers under our military guard instead of S.S. troops. One is led to wonder whether the German people, seeing this, are not supposing that we are following or at least condoning Nazi policy.

Those fortunate to escape to the free world found their suffering was ignored, subsumed in a broader narrative of the war in which everyone had suffered. The same narrative stressed the defeat of Nazi totalitarianism and the need to look to a better economic future while warding off another totalitarian enemy, the Soviet Union. Indeed, it was long after 1945 that the Holocaust began to be publicly remembered by even American Jews. Saul Bellow, who lived in Paris in the late 1940s among Holocaust survivors (his first wife Anita Goshkin worked for an American organisation that helped them), pondered in 1987 the strange fact that Jewish American writers 'missed what should have been for them the central event of their time, the destruction of European Jewry'.

Gentile ignorance of the Shoah was, of course, pervasive. Peter Novick argues in *The Holocaust in American Life* (1999) that the Shoah 'didn't loom that large' even in the life of America's Jews until the late 1960s. This influential view of Jewish American disengagement with the Shoah has been challenged, most notably by Hasia Diner in *We Remember with Reverence and Love* (2009). Diner argues, citing synagogue and youth group programmes, memorial ceremonies and efforts to build monuments, that many American Jews developed a high degree of communal consciousness about the destruction of their co-religionists in Europe. In *American Dreams and Nazi Nightmares* (2006), Kirsten Fermaglich contends that in the late 1950s and early 1960s American Jewish thinkers such as Betty Friedan and Robert Jay Lifton frequently invoked the outrages of the Nazi concentration camps, not to express their Jewishness or to justify

Israel's policies but to warn against the dangers of mind-less bureaucracy and social conformity in American life. Yet the sparse public manifestations of what Fermaglich calls 'early Holocaust consciousness' are still striking. *American Judaism*, by the prominent American soci-ologist Nathan Glazer, published in 1957, marvelled at how 'the two greatest events in modern Jewish history, the murder of six million Jews by Hitler and the crea-tion of a Jewish state in Palestine, had had remarkably slight effects on the inner life of American Jewry'. In his essay 'The Intellectuals and Jewish Fate', published in the Jewish magazine *Midstream* in 1957, Norman Pod-horetz, the patron saint of neoconservative Zionists in the 1980s, said nothing at all about the Holocaust. In the enormous *Columbia History of the World* published as late as 1972, and co-edited by Peter Gay, a Jewish refugee from Germany, there was no mention of Auschwitz or of the murder of six million Jews.

Jewish organisations that became notorious for policing opinion about Zionism at first discouraged the memorialisation of Europe's Jewish victims. They were scrambling to learn the new rules of the geopoliti-cal game. In the chameleon-like shifts of the early Cold War, the Soviet Union moved from being an ally against Nazi Germany to a totalitarian evil; Germany moved from being a totalitarian evil to a steadfast democratic ally against it. Accordingly, the editor of *Commentary* urged American Jews to nurture a 'realistic attitude rather than a punitive and recriminatory one' towards Germany, which was now a pillar of 'Western democratic civilisation'.[*]

This extensive gaslighting by Western political and intellectual leaders shocked and embittered many survivors of the Shoah. However, they weren't then regarded as uniquely privileged witnesses of the modern world. Jean Améry, who felt betrayed by the free world's indulgence to West Germany, would have known greater despair if he had seen the staff memorandum of the American Jewish Committee in 1951, which regretted the fact that 'for most Jews reasoning about Germany and Germans is still beclouded by strong emotion'. American Jewish organisations had lobbied for the creation of Israel in 1948, but few American Jews paid much attention to the new state, and even fewer visited or emigrated to it.

The most prominent Jewish intellectuals such as the economist Milton Friedman and the novelist Ayn Rand seemed indifferent to the country. In *We Are Not One* (2022), Eric Alterman shows that Arthur Hays Sulzberger, publisher of the *New York Times*, which

---

[*] Japan benefitted, too, from the American Cold War policy of 'soft-pedaling' its war responsibility, which included, as John Dower writes, 'downplaying prewar Japanese militarism' and 'sanitizing Japanese atrocities'.

is accused today of pro-Israel bias, 'forbade use of the phrase "the Jewish people"' in the paper, preferring unwieldy substitutes such as 'people of the Jewish faith'; later he vetoed all use of the term 'the Jewish state'. Sulzberger also 'consistently resisted putting Jews in "showcase" editorial positions at the *Times* regardless of their qualifications'. And his anti-Zionism became so extreme that he complained in a 1946 speech that 'thousands dead might now be alive' had the Zionists put 'less emphasis on statehood'.

Novick explains that American Jews, like other ethnic groups, were anxious to avoid the charge of dual loyalty and to take advantage of the dramatically expanding opportunities offered by post-war America. They became more alert to Israel's presence during the extensively publicised and controversy-haunted Eichmann trial, which made inescapable the fact that Jews had been Hitler's primary targets and victims. The Anti-Defamation League (ADL) still 'distanced itself from Eichmann's kidnapping and Israel's claim of jurisdiction, insisting that American Jews could not be held responsible for Israel's actions'. It worried that the trial could 'damage the image which many people have of Jews as a fair-minded and merciful people'. And it insisted the trial was 'not a case of special pleading for Jews . . . What happened to the Jews of Europe . . . can very well happen to other peoples oppressed by totalitarianism.' The American Jewish

Committee leader John Slawson urged radio and television executives to highlight in their coverage of the trial the theme that 'this must never happen again anywhere to any people' and 'this is the result of letting bigotry grow'.

Americans, too, were during the 1950s as little inclined as Jewish Israelis to see Israel as a shelter for victims. The country was largely imagined as the land of young sabras, making the desert bloom, much like the pioneering ancestors of many Gentile Americans. It was only after the Six Day War in 1967 and the Yom Kippur War in 1973, when Israel seemed existentially threatened by its Arab enemies, that the Shoah came to be broadly conceived, in both Israel and the United States, as the emblem of Jewish vulnerability in an eternally hostile world. Israel possessed much greater military and economic strength than its enemies, and had more powerful allies. Yet fears of a new Shoah were pervasive. Hannah Arendt, severely critical until then of Israel and disavowing any love of 'the Jewish people', confessed in a letter in 1967 to Mary McCarthy to feeling like a 'war bride'. On a trip to Gaza after the war, however, she recognised how weak Israel's Arab adversaries were.

Regardless, the narrative promoted in the 1960s by Israeli leaders and American Zionist groups that a second Shoah was a present and imminent danger to Jews began to serve as a basis for collective self-definition, even pride, for many Jewish Americans throughout the following decade. As Elie Wiesel exhorted them in 1967, there was no reason to think of the Shoah 'with shame':

> Why don't we claim it as a glorious chapter in our eternal history . . . It is still the greatest event in our times. Why then are we ashamed of it? In its power it even influenced language. Negro quarters are called ghettos; Hiroshima is explained by Auschwitz; Vietnam is described in terms which were used one generation ago. Everything today revolves around our Holocaust experience. Why then do we face it with such ambiguity? Perhaps this should be the task of Jewish educators and philosophers: to reopen the event as a source of pride, to take it back into our history.

Wiesel was wrong about the word 'ghetto'. It had been in use for centuries before the Shoah. In any case, he aimed not at historical accuracy but political mobilisation. In the same speech he added, 'I do not like to think of the Jew as suffering. I prefer thinking of him as someone who can defeat suffering – his own and others'. For his is a Messianic dimension: he can save the world from a new Auschwitz.' With Israel seen as protecting the Jews from another Shoah, popular Jewish attitudes underwent, Novick writes, 'a profound Israelization':

The hallmark of the good Jew became the depth of his or her commitment to Israel. Failure to fulfill religious obligations, near-total Jewish illiteracy, even intermarriage, were all permissible; lack of enthusiasm for the Israeli cause (not to speak of public criticism of Israel) became unforgivable. The change extended to language, as kippa replaced yarmulke and as Israeli (Sephardic) pronunciation of Hebrew – Shabbat instead of Shabbos, bat rather than bas mitzvah – became dominant. The presence of Israeli artifacts in the living room became as mandatory as a mezuzah on the doorpost.

Novick adds that 'in none of this was any knowledge of Israel required. A survey in the 1980s revealed that fewer than a third of American Jews knew that the archenemies Menachem Begin and Shimon Peres were members of different parties.' In *Stranger at Home* (1981), Jacob Neusner, the iconoclastic scholar of Judaism, charged that the American Jewish community had replaced its religious faith with ethnic identity. Increasingly ignorant of their own history, he claimed, Jewish Americans clung to the Holocaust and Zionism for a sense of identity and purpose. Their Americanised Zionism, as Joshua Leifer, one of the younger Jewish American writers breaking out of the houses their fathers built, describes it in *Tablets Shattered*

(2024), required no agonising moral choices: 'Zionism as American Jews interpreted it did not force them to choose between their Americanness and their Jewishness. Instead, it enabled them to fully embrace the former without relinquishing the latter.'

The State of Israel's domestic politics, or its visible deterioration under Begin, also mattered little for American politicians, policymakers and opinion makers. The US, facing humiliating defeat in East Asia, was beginning to see an apparently invincible Israel as a valuable proxy in the Middle East. Well-funded Jewish organisations started to deploy the motto 'Never again' to lobby for American policies favourable to Israel and to insist on preserving the memory of the Shoah. The American narrative of freeing the Jews from the Nazis shifted its central focus from claims of gallantry to admissions of guilt: the popular American refusal to admit desperate Jewish refugees from Germany and Eastern Europe before and after 1939 began to replace the old image of Americans liberating the concentration camps.

The Yom Kippur War of October 1973, in which Israel was saved from serious setbacks by airlifted American military hardware, definitively inscribed the narrative of the Shoah in Jewish American consciousness; it also accelerated the US's lavish subvention of the Jewish state.* As Boaz Evron described this process:

> Israel is presented to US Jews as being in permanent danger of annihilation by the Arab states surrounding it, despite the fact, which is not emphasized, that Israel is far stronger than they are, and faces no real military danger from them. Thus, these Jews are provided with the opportunity to assuage their guilt by economically and politically supporting Israel 'to prevent a second Holocaust'. Every war is therefore presented as a danger to the actual existence of the state, and the victory is presented as a miracle which has been achieved – among other things – by the support of the Jews in the Diaspora. This emotional and moving drama is presented again and again, and Diaspora Jews see that their support indeed brings results.

It did, rapidly, from the 1970s onwards. In April 1978, the television miniseries *Holocaust* revolutionised American

---

* The war was fateful in another way. Osama bin Laden dated his political awakening as a teenager to the rapid American provisioning of Israel in 1973. As it happened, his first mentor was Abdullah Azzam, a Palestinian refugee from the West Bank, who helped create Hamas. Bin Laden's earliest known speeches in 1986 attacking the United States cited the country's support for Israel. Declaring war on the US in 1997 in a CNN interview, bin Laden said that American support for Israel was the first cause.

consciousness of Nazi crimes; the Jewish equivalent of
Roots (both series had the same director), it became a way
for many Jewish Americans of forging a proud collective
identity out of a past of unspeakable suffering. A month
later, on the thirtieth anniversary of the creation of the
State of Israel, President Jimmy Carter announced, as
Begin stood with him, the creation of a presidential Holocaust commission to be chaired by Elie Wiesel.

Carter aimed to appease, before re-election, those
Jewish Americans who saw him as hard on Israel.
The process Carter initiated in 1978 ultimately helped
create the United States Holocaust Memorial Museum
in Washington. Inaugurated in April 1993, the museum
made, with its sheer size, location and potential appeal,
all other memorials to the Shoah, including Israel's
Yad Vashem, look minor and insignificant. In *Preserving
Memory* (1995), Edward T. Linenthal describes how the
new museum on the National Mall in Washington DC
turned the Shoah into 'an event officially incorporated
into American memory'. It completed, together with the
television series *Holocaust*, the Oscar-winning *Schindler's
List* and Steven Spielberg's Shoah Foundation, what the
historian Michael Berenbaum termed, approvingly, 'the
Americanization of the Holocaust'.*

---

* Among the dissenting voices was the eminent historian Charles Maier,
who pointed in *The Unmasterable Past* (1988) to the 'new contradictions'
in a 'Holocaust-centered Jewishness' outside Israel:

Pedagogic efforts to inculcate the memory of the Shoah became more intense as American Jewish leaders linked Israel's isolation and vulnerability to the possibility that memories of Nazism's crimes against the Jews were fading, or that a younger generation of Jews knew little about them and were consequently indifferent to Israel. Novick quotes the CNN broadcaster Wolf Blitzer reporting on a gathering of Holocaust survivors in Washington: how while the organisers were 'always careful . . . to characterize it as a nonpolitical event', they agreed that 'raising public awareness of the Holocaust . . . was bound to generate heightened sympathy and support for Israel'.

Trapped in the framework of the Shoah, the old problems of the Middle East inevitably lost their complexity; there increasingly seemed no legitimate grounds for

---

'Jewish suffering is depicted as ineffable, uncommunicable, and yet always to be proclaimed. It is intensely private, not to be diluted, but simultaneously public so that gentile society will confirm the crimes. A very particular suffering must be enshrined in public sites: Holocaust museums, memory gardens, deportation sites, dedicated not as Jewish but as civic memorials. But what is the role of a museum in a country, such as the United States, far from the site of the Holocaust? . . . Under what circumstances can a private sorrow serve simultaneously as a public grief? And if genocide is certified as a public sorrow, then must we not accept the credentials of other particular sorrows too? Do Armenians and Cambodians also have a right to publicly funded holocaust museums? And do we need memorials to Seventh Day Adventists and homosexuals for their persecution at the hands of the Third Reich?'

ever criticising Israel, let alone pressuring it to enable the conditions for a Palestinian state based on pre-1967 boundaries. As the conservative critic Robert Alter argued in *Commentary* in February 1981, 'to invoke the Holocaust as the supreme paradigm of the historical experience of the Jewish people is to preclude the idea of political bargaining and concessions, for every potential advantage granted to one's opponent, whatever might be given in exchange, will be seen as a paving stone on the road to extinction'.

Alter questioned the 'attempt to base collective identity on a sense of dread or – if we are utterly honest about these matters – on the special *frisson* of vicariously experiencing the unspeakable, in all the material comfort and security of our American lives'. 'In a dozen different ways,' he wrote, 'we falsify our lives as Jews by setting them so dramatically in the shadow of the crematoria. This sickly taint of genocide spreads farther than one might imagine in contemporary Jewish thinking.'

Meanwhile, events in Israel, where the settlers were gaining in both territory and political power, had a momentum and logic largely ignored or suppressed in the United States. In *Starstruck in the Promised Land* (2019), Shalom Goldman recounts completing his military service in Israel in 1972 and returning to the United States, where he conveyed his 'misgivings about Israeli policies to my relatives, friends, and school buddies in New York, [and] they expressed shock':

Though I explained to them that many Israeli Jews held similar views, they readily dismissed this claim. The American Jewish community had circled the political wagons; Israel could do no wrong. Only an anti-Semite could find something to criticize in the miracle that was reborn Israel! When I went to visit college friends in Wisconsin, I found conservative Christians who were even more gung ho about Israel than my Jewish family and friends.

Of course, evangelical solidarity with Zionism was not an expression of love for the Jewish people. The fanatical American Protestants, long hostile to both Islam and Judaism, viewed Jews in Palestine as a precondition for the Second Coming, when Jesus would save the righteous, leaving behind everyone else. Goldman describes how artists like Johnny and June Carter Cash as well as Reverend Billy Graham, Jerry Falwell and other evangelical leaders were intoxicated by religious enthusiasm for Israel. They became more comfortable with the Jewish state after its leaders openly invoked a religious millenarianism, in which the Bible promised Judaea and Samaria to Israel, to justify the building of settlements in the occupied territories.

As Falwell, the co-founder of the Moral Majority, the influential consortium of conservative Christian political action, put it, 'we can and must be involved in guiding America towards a biblical position regarding her stand on Israel'. A measure of the cynical acceptance by pro-Israel groups of fundamentally antisemitic organisations is the statement in 1982 by the ADL director Nathan Perlmutter defending his prioritising of the need to fund Israel's military: 'We need all the friends we have to support Israel . . . If the Messiah comes, on that day we'll consider our options. Meanwhile, let's praise the Lord and pass the ammunition.' A measure of the success of Christian support for political Zionism is Donald Trump's recognition, with full backing from evangelical Christians, of Jerusalem as Israel's capital. In March 2024, Netanyahu made time to receive a delegation led by Mario Bramnick, a Florida-based pastor close to Trump, who leads a theocratic movement devoted to bringing forth the end of the world.

In another dramatic and fateful shift, Israel's once avowedly secular ruling class came to see religious Zionists as partners in Judaising the land captured after 1967. As tens of thousands of settlers rushed to found Jewish cities, towns and villages across the occupied territories, a radical Zionist vanguard, fired with millenarian zeal, eliminationist anti-Arab racism and Jewish supremacism, became one of Israeli society's animating forces. But the diasporic organisations and individuals that shored up overseas support for Israel over the last half century were hardly seized by the same kind of messianic fervour.

By the 1970s, Jewish Americans were the most educated and prosperous minority group in America, and were increasingly irreligious. Yet, in the rancorously polarised American society of the late 1960s and 70s, where ethnic and racial sequestration became common amid an all-pervasive sense of disorder and insecurity, and historical calamity turned into a badge of identity and moral rectitude, more and more assimilated Jewish Americans affiliated themselves with the memory of the Shoah and forged a personal connection with an Israel they saw as menaced by genocidal antisemites.

There were a few warnings against the 'heavy wet blanket of conformism' lowered over dissenters, notably from the theologian Steven Schwarzschild, a refugee from Nazism, who charged that American Jewry had come to exist in

> an almost entirely undemocratic community; it repels and expels most significant elements intellectually, ethically, and politically liberal within that community; it brings the de facto policies of that community increasingly in line with the 'enlightened self-interest' of the dominant socio-economic powers; and it creates an American Judaism which Israelis rightly know to be abysmally inauthentic and an Israeli Judaism which American Jews rightly sense to be wildly distorted and debased.

More distortions and debasements occurred in the 1980s as lobby groups, led by the American Israel Public Affairs Committee, started to pressure politicians to stand with

Israel. In the 1984 Senate and House campaigns, pro-Israel political action committees (PACs) contributed nearly $3.5 million to Israel's supporters (one of them was Joe Biden, who, as senator, took $4.2 million from pro-Israel groups, more than any other senator in history). Those politicians urging a more even-handed US policy in the Middle East soon found the PACs funding their opponents. Paul Findley of Illinois, a twenty-two-year House veteran, who was defeated in the 1981–2 congressional elections, wondered in his bestselling memoir *They Dare to Speak* (1985) why pro-Israel activists went 'to such trouble to eliminate me from Congress? Why did people from all over the country who did not know me personally and very likely knew little of my record dig so deeply in their own pockets – many of them contributing $1,000 to my opponents? What sustained this commitment for a four-year period? . . . Surely they realized that I posed no serious threat. Could Israel's supporters not tolerate even one lonely voice of dissent?'

No seems to have been the answer to this plaintive question from the 1980s onwards, helping Israel, one of the world's richest countries, turn into a major recipient of American military aid (more than $3 billion a year, and much more during Israel's frequent wars). In an article in *Commentary* entitled 'J'Accuse' in September 1982, Norman Podhoretz accused America's most prominent journalists, newspapers and television networks of antisemitism in their reporting of the Israeli war in

Lebanon – what the Republican President Ronald Reagan himself had described as a 'holocaust'. The right-wing Catholic writer William F. Buckley was moved to protest in the *National Review* in July 1986 against 'the preposterous charges of anti-Semitism occasionally leveled, ignorantly and sometimes maliciously, at anyone who takes a position contrary to that of organized Jewish opinion'.

The increasingly volatile identity politics of an American minority was not lost on Primo Levi during his only visit to the country in 1985, two years before he killed himself. He had failed to find an American publisher until the 1980s. Summit Books, an imprint of Simon & Schuster in New York, commissioned a translation of *If Not Now, When?*, hoping, as the translator William Weaver recalled, to offer a 'Holocaust' novel to Jewish American readers. But when they discovered that Levi was an assimilated Jew critical of Israel, they stalled publication and did not pay Weaver for months.

There was another reason why Levi was a poor fit for the American culture of conspicuous Holocaust consumption. He was wary of 'excessive simplifications' of the Shoah's memory, blaming it partly on 'us survivors': 'those of us who have agreed to live our condition as survivors in the simplest and least critical way'. He had been dismayed to meet Elie Wiesel, the most prominent survivor of the Shoah and icon of its new civil religion, in Italy (Wiesel claimed to have been Levi's great friend in Auschwitz; Levi did not recall ever meeting him). In the United States, Levi was alienated by his American hosts' voyeuristic obsession with his Jewishness.

After a few days of being wheeled out to exclusively Jewish audiences, he wondered aloud to his wife, Lucia, if any non-Jews lived in New York at all. Writing to friends back in Turin he complained that Americans had 'pinned a Star of David' on him. 'I don't like labels – Germans do,' he told his publicist. At a talk in Brooklyn, Levi, asked for his opinion on Middle Eastern politics, started to say that 'Israel was a mistake in historical terms'. As he reported to an interviewer back in Italy, 'there was uproar, and the moderator had to call the meeting to a halt'. Later that year, *Commentary* commissioned a 24-year-old wannabe neocon to launch venomous attacks on Levi. By Levi's own admission, this intellectual thuggery helped extinguish his 'will to live'.

Grace Paley may have had Levi's final ordeal in mind when in 1991 she published her short autobiographical story 'Three Days and a Question' about a survivor of Auschwitz confronted by a pro-Israel zealot in New York.

On the first day I joined a demonstration opposing the arrest in Israel of members of Yesh Gvul, Israeli soldiers who had refused to serve in the occupied territories. Yesh Gvul means: There is a Limit.

TV cameras and an anchorwoman arrived and *New York Times* stringers with their narrow journalism notebooks. What do you think? the anchorwoman asked. What do you think, she asked a woman passer by – a woman about my age.

Anti-Semites, the woman said quietly.

The anchorwoman said, But they're Jewish.

Anti-Semites, the woman said a little louder.

What? One of our demonstrators stepped up to her. Are you crazy? How can you . . . Listen what we're saying.

Rotten anti-Semites – all of you.

What? What What the man shouted. How you dare to say that – all of us Jews. Me, he said. He pulled up his shirtsleeves. Me? You call me? You look. He held out his arm. Look at this.

I'm not looking, she screamed.

You look at my number what they did to me. My arm . . . you have no right.

Anti-Semite, she said between her teeth. Israel hater.

No, no he said, you fool my arm – you're afraid to look . . . my arm . . . my arm.

Recent American literature most clearly manifests the paradox that the more remote the Shoah grew in time the more fiercely its memory was possessed by later generations of Jewish Americans. The Yiddish writer Isaac Bashevis Singer, born in the first years of the twentieth century in Poland, irreverently depicted Shoah survivors in his fiction, and derided both the State of Israel and the eager philosemitism of American Gentiles. His novel *Shadows on the Hudson* (1957) almost seems designed to prove that oppression doesn't improve moral character: a possibility also hinted at in Art Spiegelman's unsparing portrait of his father, a survivor of Auschwitz, in *Maus* (1991). But much younger and more secularised Jewish writers than Singer too often submerged themselves in what the philosopher Gillian Rose in her scathing 1996 essay on *Schindler's List* called 'Holocaust piety'.

In a review of *The History of Love* (2005), a novel by Nicole Krauss set in Israel, Europe and the US, the critic James Wood pointed out that its author, born in 1974, 'proceeds as if the Holocaust happened just yesterday'. The novel's Jewishness had been, Wood wrote, 'warped into fraudulence and histrionics by the force of Krauss's identification with it'. Such 'Jewish fervency', bordering on 'minstrelsy', Wood pointed out, contrasted sharply with the work of older Jewish writers, who had 'not shown a great interest in the shadow of the Shoah'.

In 1965, when public awareness of the Shoah was still negligible, Robert Alter was already warning against an overly self-conscious and sentimental Jewishness, and its deployment by people who were 'culturally American in all important respects and only peripherally or vestigially Jewish'. Since then, the trade in what Alter called reality-distorting artistic 'contrivances – stock situations, characters, and images – intended to produce certain desired emotions' has grown. Hitler's barbarities have become, as Saul Friedländer argued in *Reflections of Nazism* (1984), 'an unlimited field for a surge of the imagination, for a use of aesthetic effects', aimed at producing 'voluptuous anguish and ravishing images'. The evidence has mounted especially disconcertingly since the 1990s.

Hailed on publication by the *New York Times* as 'extraordinary', and widely compared to the works of Primo Levi and Jean Améry, the Holocaust memoir *Fragments* (1995) by a writer called Binjamin Wilkomirski turned out to be a fraud. But the bestselling book had already helped identify a large and expanding market. In *A Thousand Darknesses* (2011), the critic Ruth Franklin identifies 'Wilkomirski-ism', 'driven by ambition, guilt, envy, or sheer narcissism' as 'one of the most disturbing trends in contemporary Jewish literature'. The vogue for Holocaust schlock, more recently evident in the worldwide success of *The Tattooist of Auschwitz* (2018), is still not as disturbing as the counterfactual fantasy of Quentin Tarantino's film *Inglourious Basterds* (2009), which represents Jews as cheerfully inhuman and jubilant Nazi-hunters in the Second World War.

A strenuously willed affiliation with the Shoah also marks and diminishes much American journalism about Israel. In May 2024, the *Atlantic*, one of America's oldest magazines, carried a piece casting doubt on the number of people killed in Gaza by Israel and claiming that 'it is possible to kill children legally'. But the fate of the magazine under an editor who served in the IDF was long prefigured by the traditionally liberal periodical *New Republic*. In the 1980s the magazine became a purveyor of racism and Islamophobia, and vigorous defender of Israel, under a new owner, Martin Peretz, who believed that African Americans were 'culturally deficient' and that Palestinians ought to be degraded by the IDF into 'just another crushed nation, like the Kurds or the Afghans'.

More consequentially, the over-identification with Israel since the 1970s continues to fatally distort both the domestic and foreign policies of Israel's main sponsor, the US. Turning the United States into the main centre for the production of the Shoah's history and memory performed some ancillary ideological functions in a political culture moving decisively to the libertarian right. According to Berenbaum, who was involved in both the Washington DC museum and Spielberg's foundation, the Shoah 'serves now as an example to justify efforts to limit government intervention'. Peter Beinart, among others, has shown how supposedly pro-Israel lobby groups, funded by rich donors from the finance, insurance and real estate sectors, today advance corporate interests and wage class war against blue-collar Americans. The interconnected 'effort to preserve

unconditional support for Israel and the effort to preserve economic policies favored by corporate power',
Beinart writes in *Jewish Currents*, is creating 'a new generation of congressional Democrats unwilling not only
to hold the Israeli government accountable for its misdeeds, but unwilling to hold America's energy, health
care, and financial industries accountable either'.

The moral and ideological aspect of the American–
Israeli symbiosis is even more striking. In 1982, shortly
before Reagan bluntly ordered Begin to cease his 'holocaust' in Lebanon, a young US senator who revered
Elie Wiesel as his great teacher met the Israeli prime
minister. In Begin's own account of the meeting, given
to Israeli journalists and reported by the *Times of Israel*
in 2020, the senator commended the Israeli war effort
and boasted that he would have gone further, even
if it meant killing women and children. According to
Begin's self-serving report, he was taken aback by the
words of the future US president, Joe Biden. 'No, sir,'
he claimed to have insisted to Biden. 'According to our
values, it is forbidden to hurt women and children, even
in war . . . This is a yardstick of human civilisation, not
to hurt civilians.'

Seeking to outdo Begin as a moral outlier in 1982, Biden
pointed to the future, and our present: the spectacle of
a US president compulsively provisioning Israel's indus-
trialised mass killing and cultural devastation across the
Middle East. But then the conviction that the old rules

don't apply closely bound the United States to Israel soon after the 9/11 terrorist attacks. 'Since World War II,' the Israeli journalist Ronen Bergman notes in *Rise and Kill First* (2018), 'Israel has assassinated more people than any other country in the Western world' – a mode of continuous warfare whose conspicuous record of failure (and tendency to feed on failure) has not thwarted the US from taking 'assassination techniques developed in Israel as a model': 'the same kind of extrajudicial killing that Israel has used for decades', Bergman writes, 'is being used daily by America against its enemies'.

In 2002, while preparing for the invasion of Iraq, US military observers closely watched IDF soldiers bulldoze a large part of the Jenin refugee camp on the West Bank. The operation that killed dozens of Palestinians showcased Israeli tactics in urban warfare, especially search-and-destroy missions against insurgents. These came in handy when the US faced ferocious uprisings throughout Iraq's crowded cities, and resorted to Israeli practices, from razing buildings and making mass arrests to extrajudicial executions by helicopters or drones. Amy Kaplan describes in *Our American Israel* (2018) how interrogators in Iraq benefitted from an Israeli 'torture technique called the Palestinian chair, in which the prisoner is secured in a painful crouching position'. 'These convergences,' she adds, 'were not lost on Iraqis, who named an opening between barriers in Baghdad "Rafah", after the crossing point between Gaza and Egypt.'

Not long afterwards, ordinary American citizens came to know intimately the techniques of counterterrorism in Palestine in their encounters with militarised police across the United States. The *New York Times* reported in 2005 that 'the New York City Police Department has worked with the Israelis' since the 9/11 attacks. According to Kaplan, 'the use of tactics transferred from a military occupation to the streets of American cities had the effect of casting the American police as an occupying force, and it may have contributed to the increased tendency to treat people of color and people engaged in political protest as foreign threats'.

Certainly, the conditions for the violent suppression of student protesters across American campuses in 2024 were established early in the century. There are many more dangers to democratic freedoms in the deepening links between Israeli governments, pro-Israel Jewish outfits and white supremacists in the United States and Europe.

In 2010, Donald Trump first discovered the political benefits of organised antagonism towards Muslims when the ADL endorsed his campaign against the construction of an Islamic centre in lower Manhattan. As president, he hailed as 'very fine people' the torch-bearing protesters in Charlottesville, Virginia, in August 2017 who chanted 'Jews will not replace us' at a violent rally; Trump also advanced the most pro-Israel policies of any US administration.

No contradiction was intended by Trump, and none exists in the fact that for years now some of the most fervent upholders of the memory of the Shoah, and defenders of Israel, are also Europe's and America's most authoritarian, and often antisemitic, politicians, movements and personalities.

Netanyahu long ago recognised the new global trends. He developed close relations with Poland's Law and Justice Party even as it moved to suppress evidence of Polish collaboration with the Nazis. He also legitimised Shoah revisionism in Lithuania and Hungary, commending both countries for their valiant struggle against antisemitism. (Efraim Zuroff, a historian who has helped bring many former Nazis to trial, compared this to 'praising the Ku Klux Klan for improving racial relations in the South'.) In 2023, Netanyahu accompanied Elon Musk to one of the kibbutzim targeted by Hamas, just days after Musk tweeted in support of an antisemitic conspiracy theory about Jewish contribution to the White Replacement theory.

The far-rightists have inherited some economic and social visions of the first generation of fascists – from constraining the rights of women, minorities and immigrants to crony capitalism. Some of their ideological manoeuvres are relatively new, however. While both Hitler and Mussolini presented themselves as guardians of a superior Western civilisation, many white nationalists aim for the same moral advantage by offloading the scourge of antisemitism on Muslims, and by claiming to stand in solidarity with Israel. Christian evangelicals have embraced the notion of a 'Judaeo-Christian tradition' invented by American conservatives during the Cold War, as the historian Paul Betts points out in *Ruin and Renewal* (2020), to combat godless communism; they use the grossly ahistorical idea not only to crusade against abortion, feminism and LGBTQ+ rights, but also to rally Jews as well as white Christians against darker-skinned peoples, whether citizens, immigrants, refugees, asylum seekers or terrorists.

Days after the rally in Virginia, in an interview on Israeli TV, the white nationalist Richard Spencer explained that liberal American Jews were helping impose a multicultural regime that allowed black and brown people to displace whites. Invoking Israeli ethnonationalism, he argued that 'I am a white Zionist in the sense that I care about my people, I want us to have a secure homeland for us and ourselves. Just like you want a secure homeland in Israel.' (Author of *The War on the West*, and one of Britain's boisterous far-right supporters of Israel, Douglas Murray claimed in 2023 that people shouldn't be stopped from loving their country 'because the Germans mucked up twice'.)

Israel's rapport with South Africa's apartheid regime was a blueprint for its present-day bond with fellow travellers in the West. In *The Unspoken Alliance* (2010),

Sasha Polakow-Suransky writes about an 'ideology of minority survivalism that presented the two countries as threatened outposts of European civilisation defending their existence against barbarians at the gate'. The simultaneous Israeli assault on several Muslim countries has mobilised some widespread fantasies of an ultimate clash between the (white) West and the rest. Netanyahu's declarations that he was leading civilisation against barbarism were echoed by his supporters, such as the editor of the UK-based *Jewish Chronicle*, who alleged in a now deleted tweet that 'much of Muslim culture is in the grip of a death cult that sacralizes bloodshed'. Among the speakers at the March for Israel in Washington in November 2023, organised by major Jewish American groups, was the pastor John Hagee, who previously located Adolf Hitler's ancestry among 'accursed, genocidally murderous half-breed Jews' and claimed that the Führer had been instructed by God to help the Jews reach the Promised Land.

Such a renunciation of political principle and moral sense during moments of crisis is not unprecedented. During the long years of Nazi rule, Hollywood was too concerned with self-preservation to take up the cause of Hitler's Jewish victims: Jews were rendered invisible, even in war films, such as *Casablanca* (1942). Many middle-class Jews supported fascism in Italy late into the

1930s, choosing to see in it a bulwark against socialist revolution and a defence of their property rights.* The present crisis would catalyse more such expedient alliances between those with minority survivalist mindsets. For white supremacy, historically exercised through colonialism, slavery, segregation, militarised border controls and mass incarceration, has entered its most desperate and dangerous phase.

The terrorist attacks of 9/11 incited, exactly as their perpetrators had hoped, an enraged and catastrophically counterproductive response. Retaliating against what it deemed a new Pearl Harbor, the United States launched another heavily racialised global war: a war on terror that presumed a subhuman enemy (even when a Western citizen) who must be 'smoked out' at home and abroad and tortured and extrajudicially executed. This war that devastated the Middle East and parts of Asia and Africa, ignited a bonfire of international laws and norms, brought the largest wave yet of terrorism to Western countries and eviscerated civil liberties in the West – finally ended in the humiliating Western retreat from Afghanistan in 2021. This fiasco, acts of self-harm such as the financial crisis of 2008, the election

---

* Shira Klein reveals in *Italy's Jews from Emancipation to Fascism* (2018) that many Italian Jews, believing in the white man's right to rule the world, also eagerly funded Mussolini's brutal imperial wars in East Africa.

of Donald Trump and Brexit, and events such as the relentless rise of China have together exacerbated a psychology long accustomed to racial domination.

'The European,' Alexis de Tocqueville wrote in 1831, 'is to men of other races what man himself is to animals. He makes them serve his needs, and when he cannot bend them to his will, he destroys them.' A social and economic order built on systemic violence turned the people of other races into an ever-present menace in the imagination of their white overlords, creating a politics and culture of fear that outlived the formal end of slavery, and other institutionalised cruelties. Racialised views of crime and national security did not cease to proliferate. Mass incarceration of African Americans, restrictions on immigration and pre-emptive wars kept identifying the dangerously lawless civilisational other: the enemy that was as much internal as external. It is not surprising that after decades of dog-whistling, politicians in Europe and America more flagrantly blame the declining fortunes of white majorities on 'foreigners', ranging from Chinese cheats, Mexican rapists, treacherous blacks and Muslims to ordinary immigrants and asylum seekers.

White nationalists, who long felt inhibited by the norms of social liberalism in the West, naturally feel a deep affinity with Israel, a state that has unabashedly repudiated political and cultural pluralism and now violates international legal, diplomatic and ethical protocols with ever-increasing impunity, even frank gratification. Pondering the broader Western attraction to the country, Yuri Slezkine writes in *The Jewish Century* that Israel – which from its inception 'rejected most traits traditionally associated with Jewishness', 'despised doubt and introspection', 'celebrated combat and secret police' and produced a 'warrior culture of remarkable power and intensity' – is the 'only place where European Civilization seemed to possess a moral certainty, the only place where violence was truly virtuous'. Certainly, the Israeli capacity for precise and swift retribution was at the basis of my own childish awe before such martial icons as Moshe Dayan. However, Israel demonstrates in its chosen multiple wars, in addition to a decline in military capability and discipline, a growing relish for violence and destruction for their own sake, with soldiers trumpeting their massacres on social media, and national broadcasters calling for the total extermination of Palestinians. It is this brazen moral and legal arson, rather than the noble warrior culture Slezkine identified, or the military heroism that I admired, that recommends Israel to many of its supporters today. There is among majoritarian movements a strong sense of identification with an ethnonational state that unleashes lethal force without constraints; it explains, much better than any calculus of geopolitical and economic interests, the stunning complicity of many in the West in an absolute moral transgression: a genocide.

But the old, seemingly irrepressible and righteous urge to exterminate the brutes must reckon in the twenty-first century with many new impediments: above all, a conviction commanding much moral and emotional appeal within as well as outside the West that decolonisation, or the physical and intellectual emancipation of the vast majority of the human population from the white man's world, is an unstoppable revolution.

For two centuries, Western countries subjugated peoples across Asia, Africa, the Caribbean and the Pacific, fuelled by the Social Darwinist belief now sacralised by Israel that a race, people or nation that did not dominate would instead be dominated, and that those who lost out in the global scramble for territories, resources and markets faced extinction. At its zenith in the early twentieth century, the brutally accumulated power of white nations seemed unassailable across much of the world. It was undermined, finally, by the unappeasable ambitions of two upstart imperialists, Germany and Japan. Then, in an unparalleled revolutionary reversal, scores of new nations revolting against Western colonialism came into existence between 1945 and 1970.

What united the disparate struggles of the wretched of the earth – and has survived their post-colonial failures – was a shared conviction that racial privilege should no longer underpin the global order. But the inequality of power characteristic of colonialism, self-evident to those on the wrong side of the colour line, persists in the realm of culture as well as international political economy. In the transition from the colonial to the post-colonial era, moral and intellectual progress has lagged far behind political emancipation. Any reckoning with patterns of thinking and behaviour developed in the nineteenth century – the ideological heritage of racial imperialism – can still be deemed controversial, assailed with allegations of 'wokeness' and rendered ineffectual. So while a formal transfer of power occurred long ago, and national sovereignty has been gained (and often attenuated) in Asia and Africa, decolonisation remains a live global revolution across the world.

It is present today in surging demands from the darker peoples for a change in the self-image of the former empires that enforced white supremacy. This involves, unacceptably for many in the West, a closer examination of professed moral values and an overhaul of public cultures, from replacements of place names, statues and museum holdings to refining of academic curricula, journalism and political rhetoric. At the same time, decolonisation has become, increasingly menacingly for Israel and its supporters, a globally reverberant rallying cry for an end to Western colonialism in the Middle East.

Part Three

———————

ACROSS THE
COLOUR LINE

The Clashing Narratives of the Shoah, Slavery and Colonialism

In the course of an extraordinarily confusing
historical period, millions of individuals have stuck
their heads into a world that they understand to very
different degrees and in very different ways.

Robert Musil

'Israel, Israel, Israel, my only happiness,' Alfred Kazin
confided to his journal in June 1967, two weeks after
the Jewish state crushed the armies of its Arab neighbours, seized East Jerusalem and the West Bank from
Jordan, the Golan Heights from Syria, and Gaza and the
Sinai from Egypt, and became the ruler of more than a
million Palestinians. Kazin grew up in the Jewish tene-
ments of Brownsville, in Brooklyn. While still very
young, he established himself as one of his country's
pre-eminent intellectuals with *On Native Grounds* (1942),
a study of modern American literature. In 1945, he
watched in a London cinema a newsreel about survivors
of the concentration camp of Bergen-Belsen: 'Sticks in

black-and-white prison garb,' he recalled, 'leaned on a wire, staring dreamily at the camera; other sticks shuffled about, or sat vaguely on the ground, next to an enormous pile of bodies, piled up like cordwood, from which protruded legs, arms, heads.' Kazin later learned of the murder of his own relatives by Nazis during the Shoah.

For years afterwards, he burst into tears whenever he read about Israel's founding in 1948. He co-wrote an introduction to Anne Frank's diary; he befriended and helped present Elie Wiesel to American readers in a major review of *Night*, Wiesel's first published book in the United States. As the years passed, Kazin became 'much more consciously Jewish, because of the Holocaust', because 'the Holocaust would not go away'. In 1967, he convinced himself that Israel 'will produce a renascence of Jewish sacramentalism . . . I feel an immeasurable joy in the thought of this, our safety, our deepest love. It is Israel that will keep the flame of Jewish faith alive. What does anything else matter!'

Such ecstatic identification with the Jewish nation, or the grand feeling of belonging to a morally special and historically unique community, was commonplace in 1967 as Israel came to possess the Western Wall of Jerusalem, and the Cave of the Patriarchs and Matriarchs in Hebron. The Jewish scholar Abraham J. Heschel, a stalwart ally of Martin Luther King in the battle for civil rights and in the anti-war movement, was one of those who claimed to have 'not known how deeply Jewish I was'. 'Israel has had a divine promise,' he was convinced in 1967, and 'Israel reborn is a verification of the promise. We are God's stake in human history.' In Israel, Gershom Scholem noted how Jewish Americans had turned to hailing Israel as the providential destiny of a long-persecuted people of the Book. 'Till the Six Day War they were saying that the real State of Israel is in New York . . . Today they have stopped speaking in this style.'

Nor was this collective self-idealisation, and the feeling that nothing else mattered compared to Israel, confined to Jewish Americans. In South Africa, Nadine Gordimer wrote to a friend about 'a kind of hysteria of self-abnegation' among her Jewish compatriots. Gordimer had observed how keenly many South African Jews exercised their right to remain silent about apartheid, and was moved to wonder in 1967 'why was it so difficult to raise money for the [anti-Apartheid] Defence and Aid Fund, where were all the fur coats and the family silver, then? So many confine their sense of justice and their compassion to their own kind.'

Over the next two decades, Kazin returned from what he would later call 'my all-with-the-Jews period'. In the journals he kept from the 1960s onwards, he charted, alternating between bafflement and scorn, the psycho-dramas of personal identity that helped to create Israel's most loyal constituency abroad:

The present period of Jewish 'success' will some day be remembered as one of the greatest irony . . . The Jews caught in a trap, the Jews murdered, and bango! Out of ashes all this inescapable lament and exploitation of the Holocaust . . . Israel as the Jews' 'safeguard'; the Holocaust as our new Bible, more than a Book of Lamentations.

Kazin became especially allergic to the cult of Elie Wiesel. As Wiesel emerged in the 1970s and 80s as the best-known survivor and most influential interpreter of the Shoah in the United States, Kazin began to see him as one of the 'actors playing the Holocaust circuit'. He went so far as publicly doubting the veracity of a crucial episode in Wiesel's memoir in which three inmates are hanged, provoking Wiesel to accuse him of Holocaust denial. In Kazin's view, 'the American Jewish middle class' had found in Wiesel a 'Jesus of the Holocaust', 'a surrogate for their own religious vacancy'. He wrote obsessively, in the *New York Review of Books*, and elsewhere, about why many Jewish intellectuals succumbed to neoconservatism, renouncing their old status as outsiders challenging conventional norms of justice and morality. As early as 1972, Steven Schwarzschild had analysed this enduring rightward turn:

One over-all cause can easily be determined: until very recently Jews wanted things that they did not have and had, therefore, to try to wrest from the powers that be – emancipation, social and political security, and national existence; now we have by and large attained to these desiderata in the Western world and Israel, and we want to protect and keep them. 'Protect and keep' are the watchwords of the status quo. The year 1967 coagulated various developments leading up to this point, and that year can, therefore, symbolize the real beginning of this new historical period in Jewish history. Barring catastrophic changes, it is a period that can be expected to last a long time.

Kazin observed the protect-and-keep mentality with distaste: 'how our social opinions reflect our top lofty incomes, and what excuses we do find [for ourselves], we who once had no trouble execrating everyone in power'. He repeatedly criticised even some of his distinguished Jewish peers for too comfortably conforming to the American ruling class. In Lionel Trilling's America, he recalled in 1978, 'there were no workers, nobody suffering from a lack of cash; no capitalists, no corporations, no Indians, no blacks'. After an evening in 1985, where his old friend Saul Bellow defended the Spanish despot Franco on the grounds that he was good to Jews, Kazin wrote in his journal about his 'lost generation': 'poor boys, "intellectuals", to their fingertips, brought up to be adversaries of power types and the "established order" – who now turn out to be voices of "privilege"'.

By the early 1990s, Kazin was alert, too, to the new

facts of American public life that threatened the long eminence of his generation of Jewish intellectuals and activists. 'We had been stage center,' he had written in *New York Jew* (1978), 'at all the great intellectual dramas and political traumas of this century.' In 1991, seven years before he died, Kazin confessed in his journal that 'Jews like me' were being driven 'crazy' by the 'sheer arithmetic of multi-culturalism, the fact that we are no longer center stage'. 'Too many other races and peoples regard themselves, suddenly emerging in the light of history (something written by the West alone).' It had turned out 'in the breakup of colonialism, that the world was indeed a very large, complex and confusing place full of many differing races, traditions, religions, cultures, to say nothing of an infinite number of holocausts not much regarded in history. This is what drives Jews crazy, that gets people like Bellow to sneer "where is the Proust of the Papuans?" etc.'

What distinguished Kazin from the rest of his 'lost generation' was how perceptively he saw the new ideas and positions that emerged after the breakup of colonialism. American ruling classes could not detect the intensity of anti-colonial sentiments abroad, in Iran in 1953 and then in Vietnam and many other Cold War fiascos, largely because, as Hans Kohn wrote with a co-author in 1971, the US had 'remained a colonial country deep into the twentieth century', never more so than 'in its relation to its red-skinned and black-skinned fellow

Americans'. However, for a Jewish intellectual like Kazin, who did not fall for neoconservatism, and felt acutely the irony in his peers joining the establishment after years of exclusion, the main signs were unmistakably at home, and menacing: a stark antagonism between Jewish American visions of Israel as redemption and the increasingly linked struggles for decolonisation and civil rights.

By the 1990s, the progressive alliance between Jewish and black leaders – embodied by Rabbi Heschel and Martin Luther King marching side by side from Selma to Birmingham in 1965 – had dissolved. Jewish Americans had ascended faster to middle-class status, and the continued exclusion of and discrimination against African Americans had spawned a militant black separatism. After the Six Day War in June 1967, as Marjorie N. Feld describes in *Nations Divided* (2014), 'many American Jewish leaders felt betrayed by colleagues in the Civil Rights, antiwar, and interfaith movements who did not speak out on behalf of Israel in this period'. These former partners, which included many radical Jewish leftists,* did not only fail to show any protectiveness for the Jewish state in the Middle East; they seemed more

---

* In an article in *Commentary* in February 1971, Robert Alter denounced radical Jewish leftists for their apparent 'self-effacement before black militancy', arguing that 'of all peoples in a world that has lived through Auschwitz, Jews ought to be the last to accept mindlessly the propagandistic black-militant usage of "genocide"'.

engaged by seemingly anti-Western movements in Asia and Africa.

But then many African Americans had long harboured fraternal feelings for Asians and Africans struggling for dignity. It was an African American who rescued Gandhi after the latter was thrown out of a whites-only train compartment in South Africa in 1893. In 1929, W. E. B. Du Bois put a 'message' from Gandhi on the front cover of his magazine *Crisis*, declaring him 'the greatest coloured man in the world, and perhaps the greatest man in the world'. The following year, he urged the 'black folk of America' to look upon 'the present birth-pains of the Indian nation with reverence, hope and applause'. In 1935, Howard Thurman, the theologian who later mentored Martin Luther King, visited Gandhi in India. The Trinidad-born thinker and activist George Padmore wrote regularly on anti-colonial struggles for influential African American periodicals such as the *Chicago Defender*, *Crisis* and *Pittsburgh Courier* during the 1930s and 40s.

The Second World War greatly heightened the awareness of linked struggles against white supremacy among African Africans. In early 1942, Padmore reported in the *Defender* and the *Courier* on Winston Churchill's statement that the Atlantic Charter, the Anglo-American vision of a peaceable post-war order, was not 'applicable to Coloured Races in colonial empire'. That same year Paul Robeson publicly denounced the imprisonment of Indian leaders by British imperialists at an

African American rally in Manhattan. By 1945, even Walter White, a resolute anti-communist and director of a mainstream civil rights organisation, was saying that 'World War II has given to the Negro a sense of kinship with other colored – and also oppressed – peoples of the world'. Black Americans, he continued, sense that 'the struggle of the Negro in the United States is part and parcel of the struggle against imperialism and exploitation in India, China, Burma, Africa, the Philippines, Malaya, the West Indies, and South America'.

Penny M. Von Eschen in *Race Against Empire* (1997) quotes an anxious State Department report on the consensus among African American intelligentsia: 'Leading Negro journals like *The Crisis*, official organ of the National Association for the Advancement of Colored People, the relatively conservative *New York Amsterdam News* and the militant left-wing organ, the *People's Voice*, conduct a perpetual and bitter campaign against white imperialism.' Early at the United Nations in 1946 and 1947 African American delegates joined Indians and Africans to indict South Africa's white supremacist regime. In a celebrated speech, the Indian delegate Vijaya Lakshmi Pandit, the sister of Jawaharlal Nehru, spoke of how 'the minds of millions of people in India and other parts of Asia and Africa have been moved to intense indignation at all forms of racial discrimination which stand focused on the problems of South Africa. This is a test case. Shall we fail that test?'

India's freedom from British rule in particular seemed to open up a broad horizon of emancipation. The day India became independent, 15 August 1947, deserved to be remembered, Du Bois argued, 'as the greatest historical date' of modern history. Du Bois believed the event was of 'greater significance' than even the establishment of democracy in Britain, the emancipation of slaves in the United States or the Russian Revolution. The time 'when the white man, by reason of the color of his skin, can lord it over colored people' was finally drawing to a close.

The advent of the Cold War with its cultures of repression and conformism fissured African American solidarity with anti-colonialist movements. An increasingly conservative black leadership argued that racial inequality at home ought to be opposed because it undermined America's stewardship of the free world. Men like Du Bois and Robeson were marginalised, and even stigmatised as communists; and their arguments that the dangers of communism were inflated and used to distract from the urgent task of ending racist colonialism were increasingly censored. In a strange turn of events, Dizzy Gillespie and Louis Armstrong were enlisted, if uneasily, as cultural ambassadors of the free world to the decolonising nations.

A new and naive discourse displaced sophisticated understandings of racism. Early in the twentieth century, Du Bois had identified racism as much more than a nasty personal prejudice. Like the caste system in India, it was a way of ordering social and economic life, the organised contempt for and loathing of minorities offering a 'public and psychological wage' to many struggling whites in American society. In the 1930s and 40s, African American thinkers had joined their non-white counterparts elsewhere in recognising Nazism as a twin of Western imperialism and racism. 'In America,' the poet Langston Hughes declared at the anti-fascist International Writers' Congress in Paris in 1937, 'Negroes do not have to be told what fascism is in action. We know. Its theories of Nordic supremacy and economic suppression have long been realities to us.' In the post-war American discourse of progress, however, Nazi and Soviet totalitarianism became the sole standard of evil; the racism of American and Western societies, which Hitler had learned and borrowed from, was taken out of its original location, the institutions of slavery, colonialism and imperialism, and presented as a case of ugly individual bigotry.

Such was the new West-is-best mood that even James Baldwin found himself arguing against Du Bois. Attending in 1956 the first international Congress of Black Writers and Artists in Paris, he wrote that what distinguished black Americans like himself from Africans was 'the banal and abruptly quite overwhelming fact that we had been born in a society, which, in a way quite inconceivable for Africans, and no longer real for Europeans, was open, and, in a sense which has nothing to do with justice or injustice, was free'.

This brief Cold War vision of the land of freedom was broken by continuing racist violence in the American South and accelerating anti-colonial struggles in Algeria and the Belgian Congo, where the CIA backed the assassination of Patrice Lumumba. As Martin Luther King told a rally in Birmingham in 1963, Kennedy 'is battling for the minds and the hearts of men in Asia and Africa . . . and they aren't gonna respect the United States of America if she deprives men and women of the basic rights of life because of the color of their skin.'

King was abandoned by his white liberal and black establishment allies as he insisted in the months before his assassination on linking racism at home to the American war in Vietnam. It was left to young activists from the Black Panthers and the Student Nonviolent Coordinating Committee (SNCC), a core organisation of the civil rights movement, to reinvigorate older structural critiques of racism. Many of them sympathised openly with Algerians, black South Africans and Palestinians. Unlike King, who uneasily defended Israel, they castigated the country as a quasi-European racist colonialist power. A newsletter of the SNCC for June–July 1967 carried, together with references to the Rothschilds' control of Africa's wealth, a photo of Palestinians massacred in Gaza under the caption 'Gaza Massacres, 1956. Zionists lined up Arab victims and shot them in the back in cold blood. This is the Gaza Strip, Palestine, not Dachau, Germany.'

That same year, Baldwin argued in an incendiary piece titled 'Negroes Are Anti-Semitic Because They're Anti-White' that 'the root of anti-Semitism among Negroes is, ironically, the relationship of colored peoples – all over the globe – to the Christian world'. He wrote that the 'Negro is really condemning the Jew for having become an American white man – for having become, in effect, a Christian. The Jew profits from his status in America, and he must expect Negroes to distrust him for it.'*

The Middle East, however, was not yet a visible symbol of a rupture between the African American and Jewish American communities. It was South Africa, the country that in 2024 became, in the face of extreme Western hostility, Israel's most resourceful and dogged critic in the non-Western world, and was already seen in 1946 as a test of post-war Western commitments to democracy and freedom.

---

* In a 1970 interview, Baldwin clarified that 'I'm not anti-Semitic at all, but I am anti-Zionist. I don't believe they have the right, after 3,000 years, to reclaim the land with western bombs and guns on biblical injunction.' He recalled his trip to Israel in 1961. 'When I was in Israel, I thought I liked Israel. I liked the people. But to me it was obvious why the western world created the State of Israel, which is not really a Jewish state. The West needed a handle in the Middle East. And they created the state as a European pawn.'

In the 1950s and early 60s, Israel had worked to strengthen economic, military and cultural ties with freshly decolonised African countries. These relations deteriorated rapidly after Israel itself became, explicitly and anachronistically, a Western-style colonial power in 1967. They achieved their nadir in 1975 when the Organisation of African Unity declared that 'the racist regime in occupied Palestine and the racist regimes in Zimbabwe and South Africa have a common imperialist origin' with policies 'aimed at [the] repression of the dignity and integrity of the human being'. The OAU resolution was quickly reformulated that same year by a majority in the United Nations General Assembly that equated Zionism with racism. The following year, the South African prime minister John Vorster, a former Nazi supporter, paid his tributes at Yad Vashem in Jerusalem.

On this visit, aimed at intensifying the military relationship between the two countries, Vorster, the architect of South African apartheid, was toasted at the Knesset by the Israeli prime minister Yitzhak Rabin as a fellow believer in the 'hopes for justice and peaceful coexistence'.*
A few weeks later, South African police massacred schoolchildren in Soweto: an atrocity that re-galvanised the

---

* The anti-apartheid activist Arthur Goldreich, one of the few people in Israel protesting Vorster's visit, discovered that the elderly man who spat on his poster had an Auschwitz number on his arm. He later recalled the Holocaust survivor telling him, 'We will make agreements with the devil to save Jews from persecution and to secure the future of this state.'

anti-apartheid movement, and its supporters in the United States. Then in 1979, Andrew Young, American ambassador to the United Nations, the first African American in that post and a much-loved figure, was forced to resign after news of his meeting with a PLO representative was leaked by Mossad to *Newsweek*. Proclaiming Young as a 'hero' in the *Nation*, who had been 'betrayed by cowards', James Baldwin brought up Israel's arms sales to white supremacists, and again charged that 'the Jew, in America, is a white man. He has to be, since I am a black man, and, as he supposes, his only protection against the fate which drove him to America.'

Visiting the United States in 1986, Desmond Tutu told the *Jewish Press*, 'You know what is happening to black and Jewish relationships in this country and part of that is due to this South African–Israel connection.' Tutu was blunter in 1989, two years after the first intifada broke out in the occupied territories, while speaking to an audience at the Stephen Wise Free Synagogue. 'If you changed the names, the description of what is happening in the Gaza Strip and the West Bank could be a description of what is happening in South Africa,' he said. 'We blacks cannot understand how people with your kind of history' can allow Israel's government 'to have the kind of relationship it has with South Africa'. By then the outbursts of black leaders and Israel First Jewish neoconservatives were making for a rancorous clash of identitarian politics in the United States. In 1990, *Commentary* magazine responded to Nelson Mandela's first visit to the United States after his release from twenty-seven years in prison with an article examining whether he regretted enough his past support for Palestinians, or his critique of the South African Jewish community.

This wilful failure to understand the significance of the anti-apartheid movement, or to acknowledge the liberation of the last big country from a racist Western colonialism, was a defining moment for a lumpen American intelligentsia, originally gathered around *Commentary* and *National Review* and now accessible in the *Atlantic* as well. But its irate incomprehension was shared by many liberal American intellectuals. These opinion makers were united in refusing to consider that the most consequential event of the twentieth century might not be the First or Second World War, the Shoah, the Cold War, or, for that matter, the collapse of communism, but decolonisation.

The word denoted not only world-historical shifts of economic power, but also profound cultural and intellectual revolutions. In recent decades, mainstream Western journalism has sought to capture the speed and scale of an ongoing transformation through quantitative analysis – China's growing share of international trade, the expanding size of the Indian, Brazilian and Indonesian economies, the burgeoning military deals between China and Russia. But these remain mere surface ripples on the spate of global change. The deeper currents have been sweeping away old touchstones and landmarks, and uncovering a world that differs radically, in all its political mentalities and emotional outlooks as well as economic structures, from the world that existed barely two decades ago.

American opinion makers were ill-equipped to understand this. Most of them belonged to what Tony Judt, born in 1948, called a 'pretty crappy' generation, which 'grew up in the 1960s in Western Europe or in America, in a world of no hard choices, neither economic nor political'. Accustomed to thinking in blocs, their view of the world rarely transcended its post-1945 reorganisation into three geopolitical spheres: the Western, the Soviet and the Third World. In their master narrative, increasingly threadbare after Donald Trump's twin victories but still being recycled by anti-communist historians such as Timothy Snyder and Anne Applebaum, Western democracies were/are permanently ranged against totalitarian or authoritarian enemies.

This discourse ably served the Cold War's political purposes and propaganda needs, but it also made for self-deception. Fixated with the crimes of Hitler, Stalin, Mao, and the miserable realities of Soviet and Chinese communism, many American intellectuals became prone to believe too much in their own idea of the free world as a custodian of liberalism and democracy, heir to the Enlightenment and nemesis of totalitarianism. Oblivious to the long centuries of genocidal violence and dispossession that made Europe and the United

States uniquely powerful and wealthy, they could not see the future, either: that the world to come would be shaped by ideas and movements occurring among the vast majority of the world's population, in countries geographically remote from, and historically hostile to, the West; that the Chinese Revolution of 1949 would hold greater consequences for the wider world than the Russian Revolution of 1917, and Mao Zedong's declaration that 'the Chinese people have stood up' after a century of humiliation by Western countries was more than just boosterish rhetoric.

For much of the post-war era, these intellectuals found it easy to discount the Third World as a geopolitical and economic force. Many Asian and African countries floundered not long after liberating themselves from their white masters. China seemed doomed to repetitive self-harm under Mao Zedong. Other countries, such as Iran, could be seen as self-destructively rejecting Western modernity altogether. Much Western journalism on the Third World mostly recorded its administrative incompetence and intellectual confusion. Writers obdurately gloomy about the prospects of the non-West, such as V. S. Naipaul, came to be regarded as authoritative by a broad swathe of the Western intelligentsia, from the Manhattan Institute to Joan Didion.

More apparent evidence of the rectitude of the Western way came in the 1990s, when China and India (and Russia) simultaneously relinquished their commitments to socialism and appeared to eagerly embrace a globalised Western model of liberal capitalism and democracy. Airy proclamations of the end of history multiplied, indifferent to the possibility a Chinese character voices in André Malraux's 1926 novel *The Temptation of the West*: 'Europe thinks she has conquered all these young men who now wear her garments. But they hate her. They are waiting for what the common people call her "secrets".' There were very few people in the 1990s like Kazin, who astutely saw the sheer arithmetic of American multiculturalism speaking of a hectic and confusing future: many more people emerging in the light of history, setting off some irreversible demographic, geopolitical and intellectual trends, and threatening to marginalise Kazin's peers, who had failed to perceive them correctly.

Du Bois, identifying the problem of the colour line in the early 1900s, had seen for himself how during the high noon of imperialism, the first globalisation, more and more people in the West had succumbed to the 'religion' of whiteness, which offered to its adherents 'the ownership of the earth forever and ever, Amen', and consequently shaded into violent zealotry. In the early twentieth century, American and European powers pressed further into Africa and Asia with enhanced force, perpetrating near-simultaneous mass slaughters in the Congo, Southern Africa, the Philippines and China. At the same time, they faced greater resistance:

the darker peoples were revolting everywhere against their lighter overlords, creating a rival racially defined identity – another transnational imagined community. In many ways, the early twentieth century was when a sense of collective belonging, and in some cases political subjectivity, came to be significantly defined by racial polarisations. In one of that period's bestselling alarmist tracts, *The Rising Tide of Color Against White World-Supremacy* (1920), the American writer Lothrop Stoddard wrote how 'nothing is more striking than the instinctive and instantaneous solidarity which binds together Australians and Afrikanders, Californians and Canadians, into a "sacred union"'. Those racial self-identifications persist. The old colour line runs today between those in instinctive solidarity with Palestinians among the formerly colonised and the ruling classes in Stoddard's old dominions who defend Israel.

At the Paris Peace Conference of 1919, a range of Asians, Africans, Americans and Europeans came together to identify and critique white supremacism. Japan, which had fought with the Allied powers, tried to persuade its Western European friends to insert a racial equality clause in the Covenant of the League of Nations. The proposal was squashed by A. J. Balfour, one of the leaders of the British delegation, and the godfather of the State of Israel, who said he could not believe 'that a man in Central Africa was created equal to a European'. The millions of Asians and Africans corralled into the

Second World War by their white rulers to fight against the Nazis did not make for a post-racial order, either. As Doris Lessing, who spent the war in Southern Africa, pointed out in *The Golden Notebook*:

This war was presented to us as a crusade against the evil doctrines of Hitler, against racialism, etc., yet the whole of that enormous land-mass, about half the total area of Africa, was conducted on precisely Hitler's assumption – that some human beings are better than others because of their race. The mass of the Africans up and down the continent were sardonically amused at the sight of their white masters crusading off to fight the racialist devil – those Africans with any education at all. They enjoyed the sight of the white baases so eager to go off and fight on any available battle-front against a creed they would all die to defend on their own soil.

Not surprisingly, Japan presented its own imperialism in Asia to Asians as a necessary punishment of arrogant white men. Many Asians, in Vietnam, Java, Singapore, Burma and India, including such later nationalist icons as Indonesia's Sukarno and India's Subhas Chandra Bose, were persuaded; they collaborated with Japanese militarists. Accordingly, the United States accompanied its effort to recover lost white prestige with the most ferocious war propaganda campaign witnessed in history. 'The thesis of white supremacy,' the undersecretary of state Sumner Welles declared in 1944, 'could only exist so long as the white race actually proved to be supreme.' Virtually all American citizens of Japanese descent were dispossessed and incarcerated, often in stockyards and cattle stalls (the relatively few Germans interned during the war, in much more comfortable settings, were overwhelmingly non-citizens). In *War Without Mercy* (1986), John Dower describes how even respectable periodicals such as the *New York Times* and the *New Yorker* depicted the Japanese as monkeys while American soldiers in Asia routinely collected body parts of Japanese soldiers from battlefields. Germany's 'decimation of Jews' was 'wittingly neglected or a matter of indifference', but Japan's aggression, Dower writes, 'stirred the deepest recesses of white supremacism and provoked a response bordering on the apocalyptic': the incineration of Hiroshima, Nagasaki and many other Japanese cities. By then, though, Japan had humiliated European imperialisms across Asia, and decolonisation could finally begin.

A much-delayed revolution, decolonisation was therefore experienced by hundreds of millions across the world as an extraordinarily stirring event, or series of events – the emergence of new nation states across Asia and Africa from the late 1940s onwards (which more than doubled the number of members of the United Nations), the abolition of racially discriminatory immigration policies and outlawing of racial segregation by the United States in the 1960s, followed by the dissolution of white minority rule in Southern Rhodesia, Angola, Mozambique and then South Africa.

But decolonisation was more than a moment or process of liberation for the world's non-white majority; it was also, crucially, a seductive and perpetually renewable promise of equality. In the very last thing he wrote, an impassioned open letter to Menachem Begin in 1980, urging the Israeli prime minister to recognise the explosive power of decolonisation, Jacob Talmon pointed out

> that the most powerful force that can impel individuals, classes, and nations to act in the modern era is the determination to oppose the hereditary humiliation of an inferior position, arising from the subjection of one people by another ... The combination of political subjection, national oppression, and social inferiority is a time bomb. Voltaire is said to have remarked that all men are born equal but that the population of Timbuktu has not yet heard the news. But by now they have heard the news, and since then the world has not known a moment's peace.

Decolonisation offered both racial equality and historical agency to non-white peoples in the United States and Europe as well as in the remote corners of Asia and Africa; it made for a particularly strong emotional unity across nations with conflicting interests. At the Asian–African Conference in Bandung in 1955, the assembled leaders of twenty-nine countries found no greater common ground than the humiliating experience of Western racism and the need to envision and remake the world anew. 'The devotion and fervor that characterized the organization at Bandung,' Richard Wright wrote, 'reduced Western observers to silence and fear.'

Many conflicts developed between the newly independent countries in subsequent decades. But opposition to Zionism remained a major point of anti-colonial allegiance, as was proved in 1975 at the United Nations General Assembly that denounced Zionism as racist – the resolution was not repealed until 1991, when Israel briefly appeared to take seriously Palestinian aspirations. Three years earlier, in 1972, Talmon had warned his Israeli compatriots of their 'ambivalent position in the eyes of the awakening races and civilizations of Asia and Africa'. 'It is difficult to expect,' he wrote, 'that the extraordinary success of the tiny State of Israel in its struggle for existence against the millions besieging it should not remind them of the success of the white conquerors in their endeavor to dominate the colored races.'

Talmon's warning was well grounded. Since decolonisation's promise of racial dignity came out of a long and continuing experience of resentful impotence, was frequently thwarted, and only partly fulfilled by national self-determination, it could keep renewing itself variously over a broad span of time: from global sympathy for the Vietnamese resistance to the United States, the international anti-apartheid mobilisation to Boycott, Divestment, Sanctions, and for Black Lives Matter.

Today, the 'spirit of Bandung' that once united new nations across the Third World seems to have faded. 'Non-alignment' is little more than a slogan. And the shorthand 'Global South' covers up much disunity and divergent interests among China, India, Indonesia and Brazil. Autocrats such as Modi and Erdogan embody the betrayal of decolonisation's original promises in Asia and Africa, and the moral and political decay of many post-colonial states.

Nevertheless, for most people , decolonisation, fusing history with promise, remains a captivating story about the past, present and future, in which they seek to recognise themselves. For decades, white Westerners claimed to have *made the modern world* – as seen in the titles of many popular non-fiction books in Anglo-America – with their political, intellectual and technological breakthroughs, and ideological and military predominance. Today, many more people have come to see themselves in an equally compelling narrative of decolonisation – one in which white men subjugated and disparaged much of the world's population and must now surrender their cruel prerogatives.

*

Many in Western political, corporate and media classes hope to quell this deep and broad consensus by suppressing scholarly examinations of racism and imperialism, whining about wokeness and cancel culture, or, like the American Israel Public Affairs Committee's mobilisation against black and brown legislators, desperately throwing money at explicitly racial causes. But the narrative of decolonisation gains more emotional appeal *especially* as resurgent white nationalists in the West robustly try to repaint the colour line, and Zionism becomes more militantly exclusionary than before.

As mobs mouthing the xenophobic slogans of mainstream politicians rampage through the streets of the US, UK and Germany, and Muslims protesting the Western-assisted slaughter in Gaza are denounced as traitors, the old affinities between the West's war-making abroad and race-making at home become too garishly apparent. Arguably, condemnation of Western powers has not been so widespread since the mid-twentieth century when most leaders of 'darker nations' were either fighting for national self-determination or incorporating their anti-colonial triumphs into the pedagogical systems of new nation states. The globally resonant accusation of genocide against Israel by the heirs of Nelson Mandela attests to the spread of a mass, outrage-inflected awareness of the linked fates of the wretched of the earth. This awareness has detached itself from the boundaries of nation states and existing frameworks of sovereignty, territoriality and national patriotism.

It partakes of a truly transnational politics and discourse about ethnic-racial crime and guilt – something that was founded after the Holocaust but now circulates much more widely, due to the new information technologies, and the velocity of news and opinion, and aims at a comprehensive moral indictment of Western elites.

Such is the power of this de-territorialised memory of the white man's excesses that the authoritarian leaders of Saudi Arabia and Turkey, who were eager until 7 October to do business deals with Netanyahu's regime, are forced to reattach themselves to the Palestinian cause. Even scoundrels know the power of this anti-colonial sentiment. Illegally annexing in 2022 four Ukrainian provinces, Vladimir Putin denounced at length the West's historical depredations in India, China, and other parts of Asia and Africa, and positioned Russia as the leader of a global anti-colonial alliance against a 'racist' and 'neocolonial' West. One of the two main financial enablers of Putin's assault on Ukraine is India's Hindu nationalist prime minister Narendra Modi, another American ally that Joe Biden kept hugging closely, who has presided over India's ever closer relationship with Israel. The Hindu nationalists barely participated in the country's long freedom movement against British colonialists. But they knew which historical passions ran deepest and strongest across the world when they accused the BBC of a 'continuing colonial mindset' while proscribing a two-part documentary on Modi's 2002 pogrom against Indian Muslims.

The significance of decolonisation – as a momentous event in its own right, and the fount of a global revolution in the identities of its beneficiaries – was always poorly understood in the United States; it explains the failure to anticipate the country's many foreign policy disasters, from Vietnam to Gaza. After a white backlash began to reverse progressive gains in the 1970s, the political energies of decolonisation came to be confined to university campuses, manifest there in demands by an intelligentsia of non-Western ancestry for an expanded academic canon. 'We are witnessing,' Richard Wright had predicted in his 1957 book *White Man, Listen!*, 'the rise of a new genre of academic literature dealing with colonial and post-colonial facts from a wider angle of vision than ever possible before.' Some of this literature started to appear after Bandung: Chinua Achebe's *Things Fall Apart* (1958), Frantz Fanon's *The Wretched of the Earth* (1961), Alex La Guma's *In the Fog of the Seasons' End* (1972). In the 1960s, the ideas that emerged during the anti-colonial struggles – of Fanon and Gandhi, for instance – also travelled back to the West just as civil liberties movements and anti-war demonstrations erupted there.

This was also the time when the rolling back of racist

immigration policies enabled more anglophone intellectuals of non-Western origin to move to the United States. It is not merely coincidental that the first major work of post-colonial theory came from a thinker of Palestinian ancestry, highlighting how Western power and geopolitical interests work to crudely misrepresent non-Westerners. Edward Said was the dandyish scion of a rich Christian Arab family who had apprenticed with Jewish academics like Trilling and Harry Levin while following the conventional path to tenured professorship; he called campus security when students protesting the war in Vietnam disrupted his class at Columbia.

He later claimed to have suppressed much resentment as a junior member of the intellectual establishment forced to impotently witness the racist caricaturing of Arabs in American academia and journalism: he was particularly offended to see them disparaged by his own idol, Isaiah Berlin. Richard Wright once spoke of this 'spell of quiet' that comes over the non-white writer 'when he sees that the point of view of the imperial power dominates the values of culture and life. The world confronting him negates his humanity, but he feels that it is useless to protest with words.' Said, though radicalised by the euphoric American celebration of Israel's victory in 1967, had to bide his time.

When it came in the 1970s, after the consolidation and international recognition of a Palestinian liberation movement, untainted by the debacles of Arab

nationalism, he was ready with *Orientalism*. In the introduction to this book, published in 1978, the same year as
the television series *Holocaust*, and a year after the miniseries *Roots* was broadcast,* Said raised the question,
'what one really is.' His answer was: an 'Oriental subject',
who seeks to disentangle the 'web of racism, cultural
stereotypes, political imperialism, dehumanising ideology holding in the Arab or Muslim'.

Said soon became the world's best-known Palestinian intellectual, and the most eloquent narrator of the
story of Palestinian ordeals under Israeli/Western domination. He was disquietingly aware, as he wrote in *After
the Last Sky*, of how Palestinians, by emphasising armed
struggle, had neglected the 'far more important political
and cultural aspects of our struggle' against a country
'which with its superior propaganda apparatus turned
everything we did against its occupation of our lands,
its devastation of our villages, and its oppression of
our population, into "terrorism".' It was largely due to
Said's work that Palestinians emerged in many Western
eyes as historical protagonists, leading a heroic new anti-
colonial movement for liberation – what people in the

---

* The dates are important, for they reveal that even as the Shoah
assumed a central place in Western collective memory – and began to
play its ideological role of obscuring Israel's anachronistic colonialism
in the age of decolonisation, and of consolidating the ethnic identity of
American Jews – it came to be challenged by other forms of collective
self-identification.

West, and in Israel, could locate in a longer historical continuum, and even identify with, if not fully support. So successful was this narrative of suffering and likely redemption – an effective counter to the narrative of the Shoah that justified Israel – that Said, by the end of his life, could claim, in an interview with the Israeli journalist Ari Shavit, to be the 'last Jewish intellectual', representing a persecuted people, and upholding the virtues of solidarity and fraternity.

Said's books were also gratefully received by many academics of non-Western ancestry: children of ruling classes in Asian and African countries in many cases, who had likewise dutifully upheld the Great Books canon. They, too, had become steadily embittered by the awareness that the best of what was thought and said in the West was strikingly contemptuous of non-white peoples, and the knowledge elites of Europe and America they admired and struggled to emulate were mostly oblivious to the worlds they had come from. Inspired by Said's example, more works of what is now known as post-colonial studies rapidly emerged in the 1980s to interrogate the free world's self-image as legatee of ancient Greece, Renaissance Italy and Enlightenment France, and to challenge the dominance of Western experiences in modern thought and literature.

Commentary was not untypical in responding to this early instance of 'wokeness' by putting the author of *Orientalism* on its cover in August 1989 under the heading 'Professor of Terror'. In 1999, the *Wall Street Journal* in an article titled 'The False Prophet of Palestine' claimed that Said had fabricated his childhood in Jerusalem, a defamatory accusation later repeated in *Time*. In 2003, a fellow at the Hoover Institution testified against Said in hearings for a House bill that sought to regulate much post-colonial scholarship. That the barbarians were inside the gates, at least of academia, had been a widespread fear from the 1980s onwards, stoked by such bestselling titles as Allan Bloom's *The Closing of the American Mind* (1987). It should not be at all surprising that, as university campuses erupted into pro-Palestinian protests, a much-circulated *Atlantic* article by the British writer Simon Sebag Montefiore claimed that decolonisation is a 'toxic, inhumane ideology' that is corrupting young minds, quite like critical race theory, a 'nonsensical mix of Marxist theory, Soviet propaganda and traditional anti-Semitism from the Middle Ages'. Encouraged by far-right politicians and his fellow plutocrats who blithely bully Ivy League presidents, Elon Musk wants to ban the word 'decolonisation' altogether, claiming that it is spawned by the 'woke mind virus' and 'necessarily' implies genocide.

Kazin himself dealt thoughtfully – and insightfully – with the phenomenon that more and more people disregarded by Western histories were demanding attention to their particular experiences: 'Everybody wants to be recognized – to which we reply, if the challenge is met at all – that we no longer have a common world.' Too many of his peers, however, didn't take well to being edged out of history's centre stage. Among them was Kazin's friend Saul Bellow, who wrote a foreword to *The Closing of the American Mind*, endorsed a book that claimed that there were no Palestinians in Palestine before the arrival of Zionists, agreed with *Commentary*'s depiction of Edward Said, and demanded to know who the Tolstoy of the Zulus and the Proust of the Papuans were.

Visiting Israel during the Six Day War, Bellow had found that 'in Tel Aviv there are ultramodern buildings, but in Gaza, within a few miles there are Arab tents that look like the molted husks of dung beetles. They are patched with dirty sheets of plastic and pieces of cardboard.' Bellow manifested no awareness that Gaza, 'hot' and 'dull', and stinking of 'fermented garbage', was populated by refugees who had fled or been expelled from Israel twenty years earlier. He disliked Arab music, too: it 'induces torpor with its endless sweetish winding and its absurd insinuations and seductions. One not only hears it but feels it distressingly in the bowels, like a drug.'

Bellow visited Israel again after the Yom Kippur War, and then in 1976 published *To Jerusalem and Back* which Noam Chomsky in a review described as 'a catalogue of What Every Good American Should Believe, as compiled by the Israeli Information Ministry'. He belatedly developed a strong desire to reckon with the Shoah, 'the central event' of the time, and admonished Jews, especially 'Jewish writers in America', for failing to reckon 'more fully, more deeply with it' – he felt guilty of not having done so when he was, as he wrote in a regretful letter to Cynthia Ozick in 1987, aspiring to be a successful American writer. But a much deferred, willed and self-conscious Jewishness as Bellow's was always prone to crash into the other particularist identities that were being simultaneously forged in the United States in the 1960s and 70s.

Already in the late 1960s, Bellow had begun to express his anxieties about the new arithmetic of multiculturalism. In *Mr Sammler's Planet* (1970), a Holocaust survivor, who escaped death by hiding under a pile of corpses in Poland, is continuously appalled by New York, which he sees as turning into 'an Asian, an African town'. Sammler, like Bellow, travels to 'conquered Gaza' after the Six Day War and hears 'Oriental jazz winding like dysentery through the bowels'. Back in New York, he thinks that America's rulers have grown weak before assertive minorities. He is 'testy with White Protestant America for not keeping better order. Cowardly surrender. Not a strong ruling class. Eager in a secret humiliating way to come down and mingle with all the minority mobs, and scream against themselves.'

Sammler personally collides with the 1960s in the form

of a black pickpocket who stalks him – the novel's only black character who in the very first sighting by Sammler, an Anglophile with a 'civilized face', radiates the 'effrontery of a big animal'. As the novel proceeds, blackness becomes the overarching symbol of the otherness, from feminism to sexual freedom and the counterculture, that threatens the social order constructed by white men. 'From the black side,' Bellow writes, 'strong currents were sweeping over everyone. Child, black, redskin – the unspoiled Seminole against the horrible Whiteman.'

At one point, Sammler is heckled at Columbia University and forced to end his lecture – this was Bellow's own experience during a talk in Berkeley in the sixties. But the besieged status of a white Western civilisation, in which Jews have been belatedly compensated, is more vividly symbolised in the novel's most notorious scene: in which the black pickpocket forces the elderly Sammler into a corner in the lobby of his apartment building, unzips his trousers and shows him his penis ('a large tan-and-purple uncircumcised thing – a tube, a snake; metallic hairs bristled at the thick base and the tip curled beyond the supporting, demonstrating hand, suggesting the fleshly mobility of an elephant's trunk').

As it turns out, Sammler is no longer a hapless victim of moral outrages. Nor is Eisen, his Israeli son-in-law, 'a victim of Hitler and Stalin' who after the war had been 'deposited starved to the bones on Israel's sands;

lice, lunacy, and fever his only assets'. Healed and strengthened by the Jewish state – Sammler notes that 'that was one of the uses of Israel, to gather in these cripples' – he subsequently comes to the United States to pursue success in business. In a shocking scene, Eisen erupts into gruesome violence against the black pickpocket before a crowd of passive spectators near Columbus Circle. Sammler objects as the Israeli keeps beating the black man with a bag full of heavy metals even as the latter lies bleeding on the asphalt. At one point, Sammler grabs Eisen's arm and cautions, 'You'll murder him. Do you want to beat out his brains? . . . I am horrified!' The Israeli retorts, with the impeccable logic of the IDF in Gaza and Lebanon, 'You can't hit a man like this just once. When you hit him, you must really hit him. Otherwise he'll kill you.'

Mr Sammler's Planet reveals much more than was intended by its author. It uncovers the explosive terrors and prejudices behind the conventional depiction of the 1960s as a time of rising tensions between African Americans and Jewish Americans.* It dares to imagine an Israeli survivor of the Shoah brutally policing, only twenty-five years later, the colour line where Jews as well as blacks

---

* Even more starkly than Bernard Malamud's novel *The Tenants* (1971) in which two novelists, Jewish and African American, living in a condemned tenement on the East Side hack each other to death.

were once on the wrong side. It also blurts out a hege-
monic elite's fear, bordering on rage and disgust, of what
it perceives as the unassimilable 'other' with its unaccep-
table demands.

Present-day attempts to suppress dissent and to stig-
matise and banish, whether originating on Wall Street,
in Texas, Silicon Valley or at the offices of *Commentary*,
come out of the same existential dread of people to
whom the world becomes each day an unnervingly unfa-
miliar place. If anything, paladins of the old domestic
and geopolitical order, and Israel, among political and
media elites, seem more volatile today than in the 1960s.
For, in the war of ideas and memory that intensified in
Europe and North America after 7 October, the narrative in which the Shoah gives unlimited moral legitimacy
to Israel has never appeared weaker.

Israel remains the foremost military power in the
Middle East, with rock-solid support among the ruling
classes of the world's richest and most powerful countries. Many older white citizens in the West continue to
endorse Israel's self-legitimising narrative as a country
built to ensure that Jews never again suffer a Holocaust. But many more people – increasingly within as
well as outside the West – have come to embrace a
counter-narrative, in which the memory of the Shoah
has been perverted to enable mass murder, while obscuring a larger history of modern Western violence outside
the West.

Talmon was already worrying in 1972 about Israel's image 'upon the minds of countless millions in Asia and Africa at this moment'. 'We should take cognizance of the fact,' he wrote, 'that for hundreds of years the position of Jews throughout the world was determined not by what they were and what they did, but by the image which others developed of them: let us recall the impact of Shylock, created by Shakespeare, who never in his life met a Jew.' Most people around the world have never met a Jew, but many may now identify Jewishness as well as Israel with ferocious violence and injustice.

At the same time, Palestinian suffering has emerged as a large landmark in what since Edward Said published *Orientalism* has become an extensively charted landscape of racist Western colonialism. Words like 'colony' and 'empire', though variously interpreted, have become the main operative terms for understanding both historical and present-day relations of domination. A widening circle of young Western as well as non-Western citizens level the charge that Israel is a cruel settler-colonialist and Jewish supremacist regime supported by far-right Western politicians and fellow-travelling liberals.

What Sammler regards as civilisation, vested with moral authority due to its opposition to Nazi and Soviet totalitarianisms, is accused of older, deeper and continuing crimes against non-white peoples. As Kazin suspected, many more people wishing for recognition now advance accounts of their own holocausts that have not been much regarded in history. A Jewish identity founded on memories of victimhood, and of belonging to a community made up of fellow victims, present or past, is aggressively challenged by other similarly constructed identities.

Atrocity Hucksterism and Identity Politics

If we know in what way society is unbalanced, we
must do what we can to add weight to the lighter scale.
Although the weight may consist of evil, in handling it
with this intention, perhaps we do not become defiled.
But we must have formed a conception of equilibrium
and be ever ready to change sides like justice, 'that
fugitive from the camp of conquerors'.

Simone Weil

When in 1971 James Baldwin compared the solitude of a
brutishly persecuted Angela Davis to that of 'the Jewish
housewife on the way to Dachau', a robust objection
came from Shlomo Katz, the editor of the Jewish magazine *Midstream*. In his 'Open Letter to James Baldwin',
he admonished what he termed 'fly-by-night self-styled
revolutionaries': 'You try,' he charged, 'to take the thorny
crown of martyrdom from the "Jewish housewife in the
boxcar headed for Dachau" and attempt to place it on
the head of Angela Davis. But this crown of martyrdom
can only be earned in one way – the way of the chimneys
of Dachau. On Miss Davis it doesn't fit.'

Such contempt for claimants to martyrdom can no longer be sustained. There is little doubt today about the outcome of a global contest between narratives of suffering. If collective memories are taken to express essential truths, deeply informing members of an imagined community who they are, and what their place in the world is, then the memory of the white supremacism of Western powers has many more subscribers today than the memory of Nazism. The pre-eminence of the Shoah among historical memories is fading even where it happened. In large parts of Eastern Europe, where few Jews now live, memories of Hitler's crimes have been giving way since the nineties to memories of victimisation by Stalin: the Holocaust is being eclipsed by the Holodomor, the sacrifice of millions of people in Stalin's plan to collectivise agriculture in the early 1930s.

Popular books such as *The War on the West*, present-day counterparts of the early twentieth century's bestseller *The Rising Tide of Color Against White World-Supremacy*, urge greater unity among white Westerners. But it is getting harder to sustain the old Plato-to-NATO narrative that treated the world wars, along with Nazism and communism, as monstrous aberrations in the universal advance of Western-style liberal democracy.

This loss of credence is due not only to the emergence of figures like Trump, Boris Johnson and Elon Musk as paladins of Western civilisation. Scholarship over the last two decades has also clarified that Germany was no exception; all Western powers worked together to uphold a global racial order, in which it was entirely normal for Asians and Africans to be exterminated, terrorised, imprisoned and ostracised. Already during the slaughter of the first European civil war in 1915 Rosa Luxemburg could see how the 'destructive beasts' unleashed by Europe 'over all other parts of the world have sprung with one awful leap, into the midst of the European nations':

A cry of horror went up through the world when Belgium, that priceless little jewel of European culture, when the venerable monuments of art in northern France, fell into fragments before the onslaughts of a blind and destructive force. The 'civilized world' that has stood calmly by when this same imperialism doomed tens of thousands of Hereros to destruction . . . when in China an ancient civilization was delivered into the hands of destruction and anarchy, with fire and slaughter, by the European soldiery; when Persia gasped in the noose of the foreign rule of force that closed inexorably about her throat; when in Tripoli the Arabs were mowed down, with fire and swords, under the yoke of capital while their civilization and their homes were razed to the ground.

Aimé Césaire insisted in *Discourse on Colonialism* (1955) that Hitler seemed exceptionally cruel only because he presided over 'the humiliation of the white man': the 'fact that he applied to Europe colonialist procedures which until then had been reserved exclusively for the Arabs of Algeria, the coolies of India, and the blacks of Africa'. Reading about the Congo under Belgian rule while living in Nazi-occupied Warsaw in the early 1940s, Czeslaw Milosz wrote bitterly of how Europeans were now experiencing for themselves 'the roundups, the slap in the face of an interrogator, suffocation in jam-packed barracks, death under the heel of a criminal of a higher race'. The historian Geoff Eley has described how the Nazis' Polish policy 'fits into the larger repertoire of practice associated with the pre-1914 "colonial ordering of the world"'. 'Europe's history of imperialism,' Wendy Lower writes in *Nazi Empire-Building and the Holocaust in Ukraine* (2005), 'shaped the policies and behavior of Nazi leaders and their functionaries who tried to colonize Ukraine during World War II.'

Many contemporary scholars tracing the origins of Nazism in Western colonialism would still argue that the Shoah was, if not unique, distinctive: racist violence taken to a new extreme by an expansionist modern state that not only sought the annihilation of a whole people, but possessed the technological capacity to fulfil its ambition, and largely achieved it with extraordinary speed and scope. Nevertheless, insights that lack this nuance while implicating Allied together with Axis powers in genocidal racism have already moved from specialist academia to popular culture. Inevitably, more attention will be paid to the continuities in practices and assumptions across the main antagonists of the Second World War.

Post-war American visions of modernisation and progress through democracy and capitalism, and a 'rules-based international order', skipped over the fact that a world war that killed tens of millions and ended with the dropping of atomic bombs had made modernity and progress seem synonymous with universal destruction. Clear-sighted observers, however, were not fooled even back in the mid-1940s. 'The atom bomb and the use without warning of this weapon of atrocity' was, the Austrian novelist Hermann Broch wrote in September 1945, 'a very grave misfortune that will compromise the "white man" and his democracy for decades to come'. In his own meditation on the war, a short fiction titled 'Deutsches Requiem' (1946) about a Nazi subcommander of a concentration camp on trial in Nuremberg, Jorge Luis Borges amplifies the argument the Nazis won ultimately by making the Allied powers as vicious and ruthless as them. Violence, the Nazi says triumphantly, 'now rules' in the 'new order'.

Judgment at Tokyo (2023), by the historian Gary Bass about the Tokyo international tribunal that arraigned Japanese leaders in 1946–8, resurrects Radhabinod Pal, the dissenting Indian judge who is a national hero in Japan. Pal pointed out that Western empires were hypocritically accusing Japan of crimes they themselves had committed – from launching aggressive wars to fire-bombing Japanese cities, not to mention dropping atomic bombs on civilians in Hiroshima and Nagasaki.

The Austrian writer Günther Anders was one of the rare voices in the 1960s questioning why those who talked of Auschwitz remained silent about Hiroshima: 'If a man can exterminate millions of his fellow men in a fraction of a second, a couple of thousand SS soldiers who could only murder millions peu à peu are harmless by comparison.' He went on to make more daring and original comparisons during the Vietnam War, writing in 1968:

> Just as Hitler gave the Jews to the proletarians, whom he had no intention to liberate: i.e. a group to which they, the proletarians could feel superior and whose abuse and liquidation was their national duty; just as that the American government gives to the American negroes the underdeveloped peoples outside of America, right now the Vietnamese. Being bombed to death with napalm, they represent today the Jews burned in Auschwitz. One can see: today's crimes and their socio-psychological functions resemble the crimes of the past and their functions much more than is commonly assumed.

The process Anders described has also been garishly on display in Israel itself, where under demagogues such as Begin violent dispossession of Arabs became the guarantee of equality and dignity for many in a Mizrahi population ill-treated by an Ashkenazi elite of European ancestry. In many other ways, the massacres in Gaza are radically expanding the old framework of understanding the Holocaust – and Hiroshima. Even as the twentieth century – that 'age of extremes' – obtrudes into the twenty-first, it is opened to fresh interpretations. Inevitably so: modes of understanding and acts of interpretation depend greatly on political and social circumstances; they ought to change when those circumstances change. Otherwise, we remain stuck with easily manipulable mythologies and unable to establish moral responsibility for acts of violence.

The new interpretations are deployed in the West's culture wars; they help make the competition for moral and symbolic capital very intense. Since the Shoah was coded as the greatest evil, incomparable and unprecedented, those describing Zionism as a genocidal ideology aim to defuse the symbolism of the Shoah and represent the destruction of Gaza as the true evil of our times. Many more people ask, what one really is, and identify themselves as Oriental subjects. Edward Said, painfully beleaguered for much of his life in his attempt to raise sympathy for the 'victims of victims', could not have imagined a time when entertainers, sports personalities and artists as well as journalists, academics and chief executives would find themselves enlisted in a furious clash of memory cultures, with the fallout affecting a range of major institutions such as Ivy League universities, Google, Hollywood and PEN America, and also the Instagram account of Kylie Jenner, who lost nearly a million followers after announcing her support for Israel.

Still, are we closer, with the renewed interpretations, to finding a replacement for the Shoah as a universal symbol of human and moral evil? One can hope that the material and psychic devastation caused by Western colonialism, or white supremacism in general, serves as a permanent warning of prejudice, and helps create opportunities for ethnic, racial and religious justice. But this seems unlikely in the short term at least.

What does seem to be happening is this: the sufferings of the twentieth century are being turned by generations alive today into a basis for individual and collective identity – a moral identity created by drawing a strict boundary between 'us' and 'them'. And it is becoming less and less clear if civic cultures can survive such bitter polarisation, or if democracy can flourish from an excessive dependence on memories of the past.

Primo Levi warned in his last book *The Drowned and the Saved* (1986) that even the testimony of survivors, 'regardless of the pity and indignation they arouse', should be read with a 'critical eye' since memory tends to stylisation and oversimplification. Levi deplored the 'Manichean tendency' in historical accounts 'to shun nuance and complexity, and to reduce the river of human events to conflicts, and conflicts to duels, us and them'. Speaking of the 'Gray Zone', Levi pointed out, in his late and profoundest meditation on the experience of victimhood, that the 'network of human relationships inside the concentration camps was not simple: it could not be reduced to two blocs, victims and persecutors'. 'The enemy was outside but also inside. There was no clearly defined "us".' Describing a cruel and conceited Jewish collaborator, Levi dared to conclude that in him 'we see a reflection of ourselves. His ambiguity is ours, the innate ambiguity of hybrids kneaded out of clay and spirit. His fever is ours, the fever of Western civilization that descends into hell with trumpets and drums.'

Such complex accounts of broad moral implication are rarely found among the combatants in today's culture wars in the West as they mobilise memories of past collective suffering that they did not directly experience or witness. The actual victims of suffering, past and present, disappear from sight, replaced by the figure that resembles the 'genocide's huckster', the French writer Alain Finkielkraut's bold self-description in *The Imaginary Jew* (1980) – the figure who has been 'appropriating the Holocaust as my own, draping myself with the torture that others underwent'. In his remarkable confession, the French polemicist described how he could identify with victims of the Shoah while almost completely assured that 'I would never be one'; how while the strong emotions roused by remembrance of a historical calamity conferred valuable meaning and identity, their overall effect could be a deluxe moral narcissism. Indeed, hereditary victimhood, as Zygmunt Bauman identified it, was likely to make people develop 'a vested interest in the hostility of the world, in fomenting the hostility of the world and keeping the world hostile'.

Atrocity hucksterism has come to flourish more widely today. One testament to the power and prestige of victimhood is that even the powerful demagogues of political and intellectual life in the West scramble to present themselves as besieged by the exponents of critical race theory and decolonisation. The politics of several authoritarian states also show more clearly how memories of sufferings are being weaponised in struggles for material power and intellectual privilege.

Hindu nationalists and Turkish Islamists brazenly use narratives of hereditary victimhood to dress up authoritarian and exclusionary politics as emancipatory, and to forge a hyper-masculine new national identity out of their narratives of humiliation, helplessness and insecurity. Narendra Modi claims that Hindus were enslaved for a thousand years, by Muslim invaders for 750 years, and then for an additional 250 years by white British colonialists – and then uses this lachrymose version of Hindu history to justify the degradation of Muslim and Christian minorities, the destruction of mosques and British-built buildings. Modi has launched a commemorative politics closely mimicking that of Israel: he announced in 2021 that 14 August will be remembered annually as Partition Horrors Remembrance Day to remind Hindus of their suffering during the partition of British-ruled India in 1947. Modi's supporters have also appropriated Edward Said, depicting dissenters as colonised minds and imperialist tools.

It hardly needs saying that such identitarian politics, whether in India or in the West, is more likely to promote rancour and truculence than solidarity and justice, moral defeatism than moral progress. It fosters, too, a state of mind that Arendt defined as 'worldlessness'. Jews, she wrote, had preserved 'a kind of eternal identity of goodness whose monotony was disturbed only by the equally monotonous chronicle of persecutions and pogroms'. Arendt believed that this self-image ended up extracting problems of Jewish identity from world history, essentialising Jewish victimhood. The new identities built around victimhood seek to partake of a similar historical innocence.

But the narrowing of identity categories results in the exclusion of vast areas of individual and collective experience from our purview; and it makes for a seemingly unbreakable political deadlock. Take, for instance, the indictment, first heard in academia and now amplified on social media, that Zionism is a form of settler colonialism, allied to Western imperialisms, and possessed of an ineradicably Orientalist and racist outlook.

The charge of racism and colonialism effortlessly gains credence from Israel's relentless expansion of settlements in the occupied territories, its pitiless collective punishment of the Palestinian population, and systemic degradation of the country's own sizeable Arab minority. Israeli leaders proclaim without the slightest trace of political correctness that they inhabit a villa in a tropical jungle, periodically obliged to mow the grass. The evidence from the past, too, is overwhelming.

The political elite of Zionism openly appealed to the interests of Western empires from the early twentieth century onwards. Many Jews in Western Europe also identified themselves with a triumphant Western modernity by denouncing as backward and effeminate the Yiddish-speaking Jews of Eastern Europe. Kafka's father scorned his son's friendship with an actor from Warsaw, saying 'he who lies down in bed with dogs gets up with bugs'. Joseph Roth, himself of Galician origin, and a fierce critic of the cultural imperialism of Western Jews, worried that the Zionists would take to Palestine the 'bad habits and customs' of Europe. It will 'be difficult', he wrote, 'for them to become a nation with a completely new, un-European physiognomy. The European mark of Cain won't wash off.'*

As it turned out, Zionist leaders in Palestine faithfully reproduced the prejudices and self-image of European elites, presenting themselves as the avant-garde of a European crusade against degenerate natives. In *The Hundred Years' War on Palestine* (2020), the historian Rashid Khalidi locates some emollient expressions of the *mission civilisatrice* in a letter Theodor Herzl sent to Yusuf Diya, the mayor of Jerusalem (and Khalidi's ancestor), in 1899, arguing that Jewish immigration to Palestine would improve the lives of its indigenous people. Herzl was of course much blunter in his other writings, claiming in *The Jewish State* (1896), 'We should form a portion of a rampart of Europe against Asia, an outpost of civilization as opposed to barbarism.'† As an early Zionist settler, David Ben-Gurion was convinced that 'it is our

---

* It didn't wash off even in Treblinka. Gitta Sereny in *Into That Darkness* quotes a Czech Jew who helped expedite the killing of fellow Jews: 'The [Eastern] Polish Jews; they were people from a different world. They were filthy. They knew nothing. It was impossible to feel any compassion, any solidarity with them.' Sereny writes that the Nazis cunningly manipulated the exalted self-image of many Western European Jews, who found it almost easier to 'identify with the Germans, whose way of life had been so like their own'.

† A sentiment reciprocated by the progenitors of the Balfour Declaration, whose purpose, according to Ronald Storrs, 'the first military governor of Palestine since Pontius Pilate' (in his own description), was to form a 'little loyal Jewish Ulster in a sea of potentially hostile Arabism'.

duty to fight against the spirit of the Levant that ruins individuals and societies'.

This spiritual ethnic cleansing in practice meant not only depopulating much of Palestine of Arabs, a mission substantially accomplished in 1948, but also civilising its so-called Oriental Jews – those who started to move from Muslim countries in the late 1940s to Israel and soon constituted its majority population. An 'arrogant, Eurocentric, Orientalist mindset greeted the Jewish new-comers from the East,' writes Avi Shlaim – whose family was forced to leave Iraq, in part, as a result of terrorist attacks on Jews in Baghdad orchestrated by Zionists – in his recent memoir, *Three Worlds* (2023). These Jews 'with their knowledge of Arabic and first-hand experience of living in Arab countries could have served as a bridge between Israel and its neighbours. The Ashkenazi establishment, however, had no interest in building such a bridge.'

On the contrary: it demanded from Arab Jews a self-renunciation more drastic than that required of the natives under British and French colonialism: abandonment of the culture and language in which they had interpreted their Judaism for centuries, and rapid adoption of European culture. During this project of social engineering, state authorities are reported to have taken newborn babies away from Yemenite Jewish mothers, regarding them incapable of raising children, and passed them on to Ashkenazi parents. As Ben-Gurion put it emphatically: 'We do not want the Israelis to be Arabs.'*

It wasn't just Ali Shariati, the chief ideologue of Iran's Islamic Revolution, who in 1967 accused European Zionists of simulating the very same racist nationalism that had victimised Jews. 'The Jewish nationalist philosophy,' Hans Kohn wrote, 'has developed entirely under German influence, the German romantic nationalism with the emphasis on blood, race and descent as the most determining factor in human life.' A contemporary generation of scholars sees European ideologies and institutions of the nation state, racism and colonialism paradoxically reincarnated in muscular Zionism, partly through the efforts of Zionists who tried to fight off antisemitic accusations of degeneracy and abnormality by forging a nationalist programme of regeneration and normalisation.

Yet it seems imperative, for the sake of both intellectual precision and political progress, to look beyond Israel's current incarnation. Just as Modi's Hindu nationalism today misrepresents the broader Indian

---

* Writing in 1959, Jacqueline Kahanoff, who moved to Israel with her parents from Cairo, charged Jews of European origin with 'racial prejudice' and 'self-glorification', explaining that they 'needed both aggressiveness and aggrandizement to defend their egos in a society where they were treated as foreign and inferior, and worse, where they were actively persecuted. In their isolation, they believed that they were the one and only Jewish people.'

struggles for political and intellectual emancipation, so Netanyahu's Zionism disfigures the larger reckoning with Western modernity that Jewish thinkers and activists have made together with many Asian and African intellectuals. It seems necessary, even while substantiating Israel as a case study of Western-style impunity, to examine the condition of powerlessness and marginality that Zionism originally sought to redress, a condition more often found in the histories of Asia and Africa than of Europe and North America, and still painfully unresolved.

Jews in nineteenth- and early-twentieth-century Europe may not seem to share much with colonised peoples in Egypt, India or China. They were a mostly despised minority within large European empires whereas upper-caste Hindus could credibly claim to represent a majority before their European overlords. What seems irrefutable, however, is that European Jews as much as Asians and Africans were trying to liberate themselves in the nineteenth century from a tradition perceived as burdensome and achieve identity and self-knowledge in a formidable modern world largely made by Christian Western Europeans.

While in the closed world of traditional society or the ghetto, they were relatively invulnerable to the racism and antisemitism that accompanied Western economic and political expansion in the nineteenth century. The psychological blow of harsh judgements – that the Jews or the natives were ugly, lacking strength, courage, initiative, self-respect and all the other manly virtues – was negligible. For the world from which such mockery and derision emerged was not considered a model of emulation or a measure for self-assessment. In the broader and lonelier vistas of the European metropolis or the imperial port city, Jews and colonised peoples lost their relative immunity to malign prejudice.

The few formal rights bestowed on them did not mitigate their social humiliation. Alfred Dreyfus, the first Jewish officer ever on the French army's General Staff, was unjustly convicted and brutally treated in prison for no other reason than he was Jewish. Max Nordau, the son of a rabbi and one of the socially mobile Jews traumatised by the Dreyfus Affair, told the First Zionist Congress in 1897 that though the emancipated Jew was 'allowed to vote for members of Parliament', he was 'excluded, with varying degrees of politeness, from the clubs and gatherings of his Christian fellow countrymen'. 'This is the Jewish special misery,' Nordau added, 'which is more painful than the physical because it affects men of higher station, who are prouder and more sensitive.'

An aspiring Jewish writer in Odessa, a Muslim doctor in Kolkata and a Chinese thinker in exile in Japan at the turn of the twentieth century came to confront a similar lack of individual and collective dignity. They belonged to a family- and kin-oriented people that had derived its values from the past but now faced an unprecedented challenge in the form of a Western modernity that rode roughshod over traditions with a powerful new racialist discourse of civilisation and plunged those not adept in it into profound feelings of rejection, humiliation and self-doubt. Even when they succeeded in finding a place within it, the price of assimilation was a painful alienation – from the past, from family, community and culture.

Their economic, social and spiritual uprooting painfully compressed the fundamentally modern and ambiguous experience of becoming a free individual; but the much-thirsted-for liberation stayed elusive after all the rapid-fire mobility across old boundaries of traditions, customs, regions and classes. It is not surprising that paths to statehood of Jews and many colonised natives come to resemble each other in their tortuousness.

Unmoored from tradition, but unaccommodated by the modern world, and fully exposed to its racist ideologies, the aspiring modernist had been condemned to precarity, and profound inner conflict, if not self-hatred. A people accustomed to living within families had suddenly found themselves, while seeking individual freedom, in a world of exclusionary strangers: the nationalising societies of Europe. As people who visibly did not belong, they were the sacrificial victims of the new secular faith of nationalism. Eventually, they too succumbed to its seductive promise: that once a family-oriented, socially rejected and spiritually lost people had normalised themselves into their own nation, a new family, they would no longer be susceptible to external assaults on their dignity and internal turmoil. Thus, in country after country, those who started by waging a struggle for individual dignity, ended up striving, in increasingly inimical conditions, for a community in which that dignity could be best guaranteed.

Like Gandhi, long a loyal subject of the British Empire, Theodor Herzl became a nationalist late in his life, out of a kind of existential necessity almost. Like Mohammed Ali Jinnah, the lawyer-founder of the 'pure' Muslim state of Pakistan, this successful journalist was deeply embedded in the secular and modern world, with little knowledge of his religious tradition, history and culture. Yet he embraced a religion-inflected nationalism as a safeguard for his threatened self-respect – revealingly, in his diary Herzl described the 'Promised Land' as the place where 'it is all right for us to have hooked noses, black or red beards, and bandy legs without being despised for these things alone. Where at last we can live as free men on our own soil and die in peace in our own homeland.'

'The Zionist movement is an expression of despair,' the Jewish Romanian writer Mihail Sebastian intuited in his autobiographical novel *For Two Thousand Years* (1934). 'A tragic effort to move towards simplicity, land, peace', it was unmistakably the work of 'intellectuals who want to escape their solitude'. As it happened, members of a literate intelligentsia, whether Jewish or Indian, were the first to suffer, in their own souls and minds, the culture shock caused by the collision of their pre-modern peoples with modern Europe. It was while seeking to overcome their own special misery that these prouder and more sensitive men of higher station formulated their various ideological antidotes.

One early and powerful common impulse among the men united by their destabilised identities and painful ambivalences under the European gaze was to renovate their religious tradition and claim superiority for it. Leora Batnitzky describes in *How Judaism Became a Religion* (2011) how one of the world's oldest monotheisms acquired its modern shape as an invention of Jewish reformers working under the influence of, and often in thrall to, European political institutions and ideologies. It is worth remembering that Hinduism, Buddhism and Islam, too, were formulated and codified under almost identical pressures. And that Abraham Geiger, the pioneering scholar who asserted that Judaism was the source of authentic religion, shares his defensiveness with the Hindu reformer Dayananda Saraswati who indulged in similar apologetics about Hinduism.

Such modernising reformers from 'underdeveloped' communities claimed moral and spiritual pre-eminence over 'developed' Europeans while trying to overcome something they were excruciatingly conscious of: their political and economic impotence, and their lack of physical power. Thus, Max Nordau, seeking 'salvation and alleviation' for the 'better Jews of Western Europe', called for a muscular Judaism (*Muskeljudentum*), and Vivekananda, the Hindu reformer (idolised by Narendra Modi), sought to remedy the ostensible physical feebleness of his compatriots by asking them to eat beef and build muscles.

The disgust with which early German Jewish reformers spoke of their supposedly backward and superstitious Eastern European counterparts, the *Ostjuden*, is reminiscent of the 'self-hatred' of many early Islamic and Hindu reformers – or the Chinese writer Lu Xun, who claimed that cannibalism was the main ethic of Confucian society. What links a later Jewish thinker like Gershom Scholem to Muhammad Iqbal is their critique of their newly invented, reformed and intellectualised religion and upholding of mystical traditions – Sufism, Kabbalah – deemed superstitious by a previous generation.

To read Ahad Ha'am's scathing criticism of Herzl – his belief that what the Jewish people needed above all was not political freedom, let alone territory, but cultural and spiritual renewal, or that the Westernised, German-speaking Zionist leaders in Vienna had lost whatever was of value in the Jewish tradition in their obsession with political state-making – is to be reminded of strikingly similar sentiments by Liang Qichao about China's radical May Fourth generation. To read Martin Buber on the value of creating an inner renewal and of seeing national unity as prerequisite for deeper unity among all peoples is to be reminded of the Indian writer whom Buber met thrice and whom Buber's protégé Hans Kohn wrote about admiringly: Rabindranath Tagore, who accepted nationalism only in so far as it opened out into cosmopolitanism. The debates about the correct form of nationalism between Weizmann and Jabotinsky, Buber and Ben-Gurion echo those between Gandhi and Savarkar, Gandhi and Nehru.

Of course, these many-sided arguments became largely moot as the twentieth century lurched down its blood-splattered path. Still, the circumstances in which Israel was born – the way the many different visions of Jewish renaissance were undermined by pogroms in Russia, rising antisemitism in Europe, and then finally foreclosed by the Second World War, the Holocaust, the stateless and universally unwelcome Jewish refugees, the exhaustion of the British Empire and the nascent Cold War, all the calamities that left Zionists as well as many other putative nationalities at the mercy of events – parallel the horrendously compromised births of nation states in South Asia: the imperialist skulduggery, nationalist opportunism, clumsy partition, war and ethnic cleansing that produced the eternally warring states of India and Pakistan. Historical contingencies destroyed at one stroke the many options of self-determination for the Hindus and Muslims of South Asia as well as the Jews and Arabs of Palestine, bringing forth nation states and permanent refugees under the shadow of the Shoah, the Nakba and the Partition.

From the hectic invention of tradition in the nineteenth to a defensive and derivative discourse of nationalism and then compromised statehood in the mid-twentieth century: these are some historical frameworks of Asia and Africa in which Israel can be productively accommodated. Certainly, the role of settler-Zionist ideology in the creation of Israel should not be exaggerated. Not until after the war did it attract more than a trickle of Jews to Palestine. Even the broader sentiment in favour of a Jewish homeland grew stronger only after the murder of six million Jews in Europe was revealed, along with a continuing deficit of compassion in the West. There are also other ways to avoid the temptation of reducing history to an endless agon between evil perpetrator and innocent victim, or the binarism of colonialism and anti-colonialism.

Post-colonial studies emerged mostly in the West, primarily concerned with how Western power shaped the representation of non-Westerners during the colonial period. This critique of the West doesn't always take into account how the language of anti-colonialism was co-opted – and compromised – by demagogic post-colonial rulers. Nor does it cover with much depth the political and economic experimentation in many societies in Asia and Africa after liberation from colonialism – what often exposed them to more insidious forms of external exploitation and internal corruption. For Israel also came to resemble any number of Asian and African states with the programme of state-building, territorial consolidation and nationalist myth-making it launched after 1948. India's most prominent socialist leaders in the 1950s – J. P. Narayan, J. B. Kripalani and Asoka Mehta – visited Israel, breaking the diplomatic boycott of the country by their government, and spoke highly of what they saw as a programme of socialist modernisation.

Living undercover in Cairo in the 1950s, Ahmed Ben Bella, leader of the National Liberation Front who later became the first prime minister of the Algerian Republic, closely followed the work of trade unions, kibbutzim and other social institutions in Israel. He told his Jewish landlords that Israel was a 'civilization of the avant-garde', an inspiring example for an independent Algeria to follow while addressing its economic and social problems.*

Another of Israel's more unusual admirers was the Iranian thinker Jalal Al-e-Ahmad. Al-e-Ahmad recognised that 'Israel is a coarsely realized indemnity for the

---

* The story is told by Kahanoff, the daughter of the landlords, in *Mongrels or Marvels* (2011).

Fascists' sins in Dachau, Buchenwald, and the other death camps during the war'. 'Pay close attention,' he wrote, 'that is the West's sin and I, an Easterner, am paying the price.' Yet he came away in 1963 from a visit to Yad Vashem in tears, and with the conviction that the Jewish state was the best response to a tortured history of the Jews. Moreover, its expedient nation-building through public education, Hebrew-language instruction and collectivist industry was a useful model for those aspiring to build a strong Islamic state: 'Israel is the best of all exemplars of how to deal with the West, how with the spiritual force of martyrdom we can milk its industry, demand and take reparations from it and invest its capital in national development, all for the price of a few short days of political dependence, so that we can solidify our new enterprise.'

In the autumn of 1964, shortly after Jalal Al-e-Ahmad published his impressions of Israel, he received a phone call from a 25-year-old seminary student. Two years previously, Al-e-Ahmad had published *Gharbzadegi* ('Westoxification'), a scathing attack on the pro-Western regime of Shah Mohammad Reza Pahlavi; it had made him an intellectual hero to the shah's religious opposition. The seminary student later recalled how, as he spoke to Al-e-Ahmad on the phone, 'the intelligence, affection, purity, and suffering of a man who in those days was at the pinnacle of opposition literature crashed over me like a wave'. Nevertheless, the aspiring cleric was frank with Al-e-Ahmad. The article's praise of Israel had caused great distress to both him, Ali Khamenei, Iran's supreme leader today, and his mentor, Ayatollah Ruhollah Khomeini.

The ideologues of Hindu nationalism were much less divided in their admiration for Israel. Indeed, India's unexpected post-colonial evolution from a socialistic and secular political culture to Hindu supremacism during a global regime of neo-liberalism should alert us to the many different matrices of power other than colonialism and anti-colonialism. Internal developments within India and Israel, from the reclaiming of religious sites (Ayodhya, Jerusalem, Hebron) to socio-economic and political realignments, again tell another significant story that is excluded by the competing narratives of hereditary victimhood.

The nationalisms of India and Israel acquire an overtly religious and millenarian dimension at around the same time, as unrest grows in the occupied territories and Kashmir in the 1980s, and the two post-colonial states resort to repressive methods that even Western colonialists mostly eschewed. Then, in the 1990s, both countries embark on a deeper economic and ideological makeover – the rejection of the ideals of inclusive growth and egalitarianism in favour of Reaganite–Thatcherite notions about private wealth creation. Small economic booms follow hectic privatisation, liberalisation and decimation of the welfare state, but economic inequality deepens unmanageably. In India and Israel as much as anywhere else, uneven economic growth has helped create fierce new constituencies, among haves as well as have-nots, for xenophobia, and ultra-nationalist demagogues have duly emerged, ranting about internal and external enemies and capturing democratic institutions.

The recent history of the two countries falls into a globalised pattern of authoritarian populism and demagoguery. In a world where unruly economic flows compromise national sovereignty, the old fantasies of cultural purification and ethnic-racial unity have grown stronger. Yet again, in a grim reprise of the history of modern antisemitism, minorities bear the brunt of the fears and anxieties provoked by real or imagined marginality in a bewilderingly enlarged and incomprehensible world. Ethnic-racial prejudice, it has become clear, is an enduringly potent and mercurial political force of modernity. Inseparable from both nationalism and capitalism, it flourishes on all sides of the old colour line, and devours fresh victims all the time: European Jews, Asians and Africans yesterday, Muslims and immigrants today.

It has become particularly treacherous in the West, where the steady erosion of the inherited privileges of whiteness, and assertiveness of previously marginal peoples, has panicked many individuals and institutions into crude and reckless exertions of arbitrary power. This panic, caused by the spectre of impoverished and needy masses of non-Western ancestry, publicly expressed fears about immigration, Islamic fundamentalism and population explosions, or through a racialised vocabulary ('welfare queens', 'super-predators'), has been building up for some decades.

The world of individual rights, open frontiers and international law is now receding fast. Today, the US fence along its Mexican border, the Australian practice of imprisoning asylum seekers on offshore islands, the German promise of mass deportations, the open incitement by a British home secretary of far-right English nationalists, and the growing obsession of many young men with 'white genocide', 'the Great Replacement' and other end-time scenarios of the early twenty-first century, make cruelly visible the homecoming of white supremacism at the heart of the modern West.

Its fierce fortress mentalities were inflamed on 7 October 2023, when Hamas destroyed, permanently, Israel's aura of invulnerability. The surprise assault by people presumed to have been crushed represents, after 9/11, the twenty-first century's second Pearl Harbor to many shocked and horrified white majoritarians. And, as before, the perception among them that white power has been publicly violated has 'triggered', in John Dower's words, 'a rage bordering on the genocidal'.

Trying to regain their image of potency through an extensive bloodbath, Israel and its supporters today lurch towards the 'terrible probability' James Baldwin once outlined: that the winners of history, 'struggling to hold on to what they have stolen from their captives, and unable to look into their mirror, will precipitate a chaos throughout the world which, if it does not bring life on this planet to an end, will bring about a racial war such as the world has never seen'. We have already witnessed in Gaza – after the millions of avoidable deaths in the pandemic – another stage of what the social anthropologist Arjun Appadurai calls 'a vast worldwide Malthusian correction' that is 'geared to preparing the world for the winners of globalisation, minus the inconvenient noise of its losers'.

It is no exaggeration to say that the ethical and political stakes have rarely been higher. The atrocities of Gaza, sanctioned, even sanctified, by the free world's political and media class, and brashly advertised by its perpetrators, have not only devastated an already feeble belief in social progress. They challenge, too, a fundamental assumption that human nature is intrinsically good, capable of empathy. At the same time, as the memory of the Shoah contends with memories of slavery and imperialism, the Native American and Armenian genocides and other calamities, it is becoming increasingly unclear if these clashing cultures of memory can yield a useful lesson for the present, and throw fresh light on its problems, let alone offer practicable solutions. Nor do rigorously historicised versions of those memories seem an improvement; they are likely to remain antagonistic, supporting the spiral of tribal hatred.

Is it possible to rescue visions of justice and solidarity from zero-sum contests for recognition and identity, and the strange quests for guiltlessness? In the face of Gaza, we ought to do more than register anger, grief, disgust or guilt; neither veneration of the victims nor loathing of the perpetrators will help us see a way out of a global impasse. Is it possible to imagine moral and political action in the present that is liberated from Manichaean historical narratives?

The questions have more urgency today because billions of people have become politically conscious around the world only to confront a sinisterly uncovered Janus face of modernity: how while making possible progress and freedom, it simultaneously inflicts new forms of regression and enslavement; how barbarism and civilisation, far from being opposed, are inseparably entangled.

It is also their fate to recognise that the utopian imaginings of the last century, which gave purpose and shape to innumerable lives, have been used up. Few of us believe any more in socialist revolution, the flat world of capitalist globalisation, or, for that matter, the 'China Model' of state-led development. The new utopias on offer from Silicon Valley's tycoons seem technologically overdetermined, with no scope for moral action.

Helpless before the future, we still feverishly hope to use our particular understanding of the past to shape it; it is one of the chief ways to keep alive the idea of individual agency. But is it possible both to remember the past and to look to a future in which we are not exclusively concerned with, as Nadine Gordimer worried in 1967, our own kind?

Gordimer was right to worry. Choosing to make Israel and the uniqueness of the Shoah a pillar in their collective identity, many Jewish South Africans became committed to downplaying apartheid. A general secretary of the South African Jewish Board of Deputies (SAJBD) could write to B'nai B'rith challenging 'the assumption that everything about apartheid is evil – that any form of segregation or racial discrimination is wrong'; he could argue that such a view reflected 'little or nothing of the real complexities in the relationship between a white minority and a large non-white majority, differing greatly in their standards of civilisation, etc.'. On his return from Yad Vashem in 1976, the formerly pro-Nazi South African prime minister Vorster was honoured with a banquet in Cape Town by the SAJBD.

In a 1993 speech, Nelson Mandela expressed an enduring public sentiment: 'the people of South Africa will never forget the support of the state of Israel to the apartheid regime'. Mandela was critical, too, of Jewish organisations in South Africa. But South Africa's history also reveals a continuous and unselfconscious blurring of the colour line – and this wasn't achieved by the brave Jewish comrades of Mandela alone. Take Ahmed Kathrada, one of Mandela's close confidants and his fellow inmate on Robben Island.

Born in 1929 in a small town about 150 miles from Johannesburg into a Muslim family of Indian descent, Kathrada lived through the rapid consolidation of the apartheid regime from the late 1940s onwards, when Afrikaners, who had unabashedly supported the Nazis, introduced repressive laws. As a young member of the Communist Party, he visited the East European sites of Nazi atrocities in 1951 – probably one of the earliest non-Westerners to do so. Two years previously, W. E. B. Du Bois had come away from the ruins of the Warsaw Ghetto with a deeper understanding of the different but analogous historical experiences of Jews and blacks: 'the problem of slavery, emancipation, and caste in the United States was no longer in my mind a separate and unique thing as I had so long conceived it'. Indeed, 'the race problem in which I was interested cut across lines of color and physique and belief and status and was a matter of cultural patterns, perverted teaching and human hate and prejudice, which reached all sorts of people and caused endless evil to all men'.

Du Bois was expressing in nascent form an idea that the British critic Stuart Hall later refined: the idea of race as a 'sliding signifier', which is not connected in any

simple way to biological classifications, and is an ideologically flexible category for defining the lawless other
as opposed to real citizens with rights. Kathrada reached
independently the same view of race as a marker of
inferior status after visiting the Warsaw Ghetto and Auschwitz. Back in South Africa, he frequently invoked in
his speeches Jewish suffering under the Nazi regime,
comparing Hitler's ghettoising of Jews in Poland with
the apartheid regime's brutally segregationist measures.

Arrested in 1963 at Rivonia along with other ANC
members plotting Mandela's liberation, Kathrada found
that one of the books smuggled into the prison at
Robben Island was *The Diary of Anne Frank*. He read and
reread the book, and shared and discussed it with fellow
inmates; he also secretly copied the passages that most
inspired him into his notebook. Some of these passages
are dated 11 April 1944, and refer to Frank's expecta-
tions of the time when she and her family will not be
defined as Jews: 'We have been pointedly reminded that
we are in hiding, that we are Jews in chains, chained
to one spot, without any rights, but with a thousand
duties. Surely, the time will come when we are people
again, and not just Jews.'

After the end of apartheid, when ANC leaders variously honoured their invigorating encounters with Anne
Frank on Robben Island, Kathrada amplified her claim
to a humanity beyond ascribed identities; he compared
the refuge given to Anne Frank to the sheltering of

black fugitives by white families and the selfless work of Jewish activists such as Ruth First and Joe Slovo. Things were much worse for Anne Frank, he insisted. Yet the experiences of a Muslim victim of racial colonialism on Robben Island and a Jewish girl hiding in Nazi-occupied Amsterdam were not incommensurate. Rather than regarding his own experience as 'a separate and unique thing', and basing his separate and unique identity on it – a move many pro-Israel South African Jews made – Kathrada brought the long struggles for decolonisation and civil rights into a conversation with the Jewish trauma.

Conventional histories by their very nature exclude such conjunctures when people break free from comforting affiliations to nation, race and civilisation to acknowledge a mutual vulnerability with those deemed, often by those very same histories, as their 'others'. There is, the historian Marc David Baer writes in *German, Jew, Muslim, Gay: The Life and Times of Hugo Marcus* (2020), an account of an influential Jewish convert to Islam, a 'growing body of literature focusing on the "lost stories" of European Muslims and Muslims of Europe who saved Jews from Nazi persecution'. Little is still known about the sympathies of Shmuel Hugo Bergmann and Josef Horowitz, prominent Jewish intellectuals in Palestine, with anti-colonial politics in India, or how Leopold Weiss, a Ukrainian Jew educated in

Vienna, became Pakistan's representative at the United Nations in the early 1950s.

In her forthcoming book on the Jewish Bundist movement in Eastern Europe, Molly Crabapple excavates a cable sent by Bundists from the Warsaw Ghetto in 1942, imploring Winston Churchill to release Gandhi from prison in India:

> Underground Jewish Labor Movement in Poland in tragic days of annihilation of entire Jewish population by German conquerors considers it her sacred duty to share request of freedom loving elements throughout the world to release Mohandas Gandhi most prominent leader of people of India who are striving to liberate their country.

These affiliations that cut across politically defined borders are potential triggers of what Michael Rothberg calls 'multidirectional memory' – what brings previously separated histories together, uncovering a broader vista of human fraternity and solidarity than the national or ethnic-racial community, and a greater range of modernity's victims. They are mostly visible in 'marginalised texts', such as Kathrada's annotations of Anne Frank's diary, the above cable sent to Churchill by Warsaw's Bundists, 'or in marginal moments of well-known texts'. There are some such underexplored moments also in *Mr Sammler's Planet* when the rigid lines between white and black, Jew and goy, West and non-West, coloniser and colonised, victim and victimisers are blurred.

Bellow's novel, written in the wake of the Six Day War, was heavily attacked for its outbursts against multicultural New York and the political upsurges of the 1960s. The novel does seem, as I wrote earlier, obsessed with blackness, and African Americans' evidently primeval threat to a civilisation that has finally accommodated Jews – a threat met with extreme violence from the Israeli who beats Sammler's black stalker. Bellow's own journey from Trotskyism to Palestine-denialism might seem to confirm the politically hostile readings of his novel. But novels often exceed their author's conscious intentions and obsessions. And *Mr Sammler's Planet* turns out to be on closer reading no simple tale of a Holocaust survivor assuming the prejudices of white Americans, or seeking protection from the hypermasculine Israeli.

Far from being a paranoid victim of the Shoah, drifting into bigotry, Sammler is an active agent, capable of moral perception and choice. He visits Gaza after 1967 and sees the 'unburied Arab bodies' that have 'roasted in the sun' and the dogs that eat the 'human roast'; he notices the Israeli soldiers casually playing football amid the carnage. This is of course the time after the Six Day War when, as Thomas Friedman put it, 'American Jews pored over the headlines, watched all the television footage of Israeli soldiers swimming in the Suez Canal, and said to themselves, "My God, look who we are! We have power! We do not fit the Shylock image, we are ace pilots; we are not the cowering timid Jews who get sand kicked in their faces, we are tank commanders."'

'These Jews were tough,' Sammler concedes while looking at rotting Arab corpses on Israel's newly occupied lands. But he cannot participate in any jubilant American celebrations of the indomitable new Jew. He is not only a survivor of the Shoah who literally clawed his way out of a ditch full of corpses in Poland, including that of his wife. He also knows what it is to unfeelingly commit murder. Bellow describes how, while hiding in a forest, Sammler captured a German soldier and killed him in cold blood as the latter pleaded for his life.

> To kill the man he ambushed in the snow had given him pleasure. Was it only pleasure? It was more. It was joy. You would call it a dark action? On the contrary, it was also a bright one. It was mainly bright. When he fired his gun, Sammler, himself nearly a corpse, burst into life. Freezing in Zamosht Forest, he had often dreamed of being near a fire. Well, this was more sumptuous than fire. His heart felt lined with brilliant, rapturous satin. To kill the man and to kill him without pity, for he was dispensed from pity.

Sammler knows how quickly the victim can turn into an inhuman victimiser and succumb to 'the idea that one could recover, or establish, one's identity by killing, becoming equal thus to any, equal to the greatest'. He sees his Israeli son-in-law Eisen preparing to assault the black pickpocket, and notices that 'there was something limitless, unbounded, about the way he squared off, took the man's measure, a kind of sturdy viciousness. Everything went into that blow, discipline, murderousness, everything.' The survivalist's brute logic – the logic of Israel's destruction of Gaza – and the reminder of his own past and present complicity in murderous violence sinks Sammler's heart – 'completely'. And it expels him to Primo Levi's Gray Zone – the area where the space between victims and perpetrators shrinks, the lines dividing evil from innocence are blurred, moral responsibility has to be assumed by the unfortunate, and the guilt of implication is crushing. There are, finally, too many unbearable historical echoes for Sammler in a scene where a now privileged Jew watches, together with a crowd of passive bystanders, an Israeli crushing the skull of a black man. He recoils in disgust from Eisen, a 'homicidal maniac', who belongs 'in the mental hospital'.

The black man remains a cipher to the end, reduced by Bellow to an object of specifically Jewish anxieties, and acknowledged as a human being deserving of sympathy only after he is mutilated by a maniac. Yet Sammler defies Israel's eliminationist kill-or-be-killed version of Never Again, rejecting the political and moral degradations deemed necessary for his safety. He might not be ready, as Simone Weil urged, 'to change sides, like Justice, that fugitive from the camp of conquerors'. But he has survived, unlike Anne Frank, to know the time when Jews can be people again, and not just Jews; the time, also, when the victims of modernity are not primarily Jews. And, perhaps, in that survivor's intuition of an indivisible suffering, we can begin to look for ways to reconcile the clashing narratives of the Shoah, slavery and colonialism.

Epilogue

Hope in a Dark Time

> Isn't it true that the voices among us speaking of
> conscience and good are growing stronger?
> Nadezhda Mandelstam, *Hope Against Hate*

Gaza has lengthened the shadow of the Shoah over many
more people than the world's Jewish population. It
has been the fate of billions across the world to know
the death instinct at work in modern history. Isolated
moments from an orgy of bestial violence will long
flicker in their memories: Sha'ban al-Dalou, a 19-year-old
engineering student, burning alive, with an IV line connected to his arm, in one of the many hospitals bombed
by Israel; Israeli soldiers, interviewed by CNN, claiming
they can 'no longer eat meat' after crushing hundreds of
Palestinians under bulldozers, and noticing how 'everything squirts out'. Forcing into our consciousness the
gratuitous violence of our societies, such an incomprehensible offence is incurable, as Primo Levi warned. It
can only 'spring up in a thousand ways, against the very

will of all, as a thirst for revenge, as moral breakdown, as negation, as weariness, as resignation'. And it will make harder the urgent ethical task of linking the different histories of suffering to each other, of exploring together a collectively calamitous past – what can orient us to challenges of an inescapably pluralist future and the common fate of climate change.

After witnessing savage mass murder over several months, with the knowledge that it was conceived, executed and endorsed by people much like themselves, who presented it as a collective necessity, legitimate and even humane, millions now feel less at home in the world. The shock of this renewed exposure to a peculiarly modern evil – the evil done in the pre-modern era only by psychopathic individuals and unleashed in the last century by rulers and citizens of rich and supposedly civilised societies – cannot be overstated. Nor can the moral abyss we confront.

The twentieth century – marked by the most brutal conflicts and the biggest moral cataclysms in history – exposed the dangers of a world where no ethical constraint existed over what human beings could do or dared to do. Secular reason and modern science, which displaced and replaced traditional religion, not only revealed their incapacity to legislate human conduct, they were also implicated in the new and efficient modes of slaughter demonstrated by Auschwitz and Hiroshima. Principled religious commitments were in decline everywhere. But in the decades of reconstruction after 1945, it was possible, even imperative, to hope that organised human viciousness was broadly in retreat. One could at least try to cling to the negative secular theology, 'Never Again' espoused in commemorations of the Shoah, even if it was frequently repudiated in Cambodia, Rwanda and the Balkans.

The profound rupture we feel today is a final rupture in the moral history of the world since the ground zero of 1945 – the history in which the Shoah was a universal reference for a calamitous breakdown of human morality.

For some time now, our exalted ideas about our countries, whether in India, Israel, the United States or Europe, have been in a state of collapse. The world as we have known it, moulded since 1945 by the beneficiaries of slavery, colonialism and anti-colonial nationalism, has been crumbling. Far-right mobilisations in the United States, France and United Kingdom, as well as in the former Axis powers of Germany and Italy, speak of an irreversible crisis; the scapegoating of minorities – immigrants, Muslims, trans people – threatens a recrudescence of the pathologies of modernity that blighted the first half of the twentieth century. Yet again political, corporate and media institutions show, this time across a broader swathe, a contemptuous face to individual conscience, to judgements of right and wrong.

In the East as well as the West, the Global North and

the Global South, we have been called to fresh struggles for freedom, equality and dignity, and to create a world with less misery. But it is Gaza that has pushed many to a genuine reckoning with the deep malaise of their societies.

It is Gaza that has quickened their understanding of a decrepit world which no longer has any belief in itself, and which, concerned merely with self-preservation, tramples freely on the rights and principles it once held sacred, repudiates all sense of dignity and honour, and rewards violence, lies, cruelty and servility.

At the same time that Gaza induces vertigo, a feeling of chaos and emptiness, it becomes for countless powerless people the essential condition of political and ethical consciousness in the twenty-first century – just as the First World War was for a generation in the West.

The crimes in Gaza and the many enabling acts close to home of collusion and wilful indifference have had the deepest imprint among young people in their late teens and early twenties. On the cusp between childhood and adulthood, they have received a brutal and quick education in history's barbarities, and how the grown-ups in charge excuse and justify them: an experience wholly foreign to their collective experience thus far. As politicians, bureaucrats, businessmen and journalists lied and obfuscated, or pretended ignorance, young students were left to deal in real time with a maddening phenomenon that historians of genocides tackle retrospectively, and are still struggling with: 'the vexed issue of bystand-ing', as Mary Fulbrook describes it in *Bystander Society* (2023), 'of standing passively by, failing to intervene and assist victims, effectively condoning violence by not standing up to condemn it, even sustaining the perpetra-tor side by appearing to support public demonstrations of violence'.

Erupting into protests, young people have faced, espe-cially in the United States, the full force of condemnation by their powerful elders, whether the university admin-istrators unleashing militarised police against them, the billionaires obliterating their job opportunities, or the presidential candidate promising to deport the foreign-ers among them. Their often vehement and exclusionary rhetoric won't advance the necessary work of mapping affinities, building bridges across antagonistic memory cultures, and acknowledging an indivisible suffering. But one does not have to endorse all of their positions and tactics, or condone their occasionally intolerant fringe, to appreciate the depth of their rejection of conventional power, or to recognise that their refusal to become col-laborators in violence and injustice is truly rare.

In *The Drowned and the Saved*, Primo Levi describes Auschwitz as 'the macrocosm of totalitarian society', in which 'power is conceded generously, independent of ability and merit, to those who are willing to defer to hierarchical authority and thereby win an other-wise unattainable social promotion'. Levi then swerves unexpectedly to question if the 'broad band of gray consciences that stands between the potentates of evil and the pure victims' is peculiar to a totalitarian regime. He wonders, darkly, whether the collaborator with Nazis is more akin to us than we like to think, because 'we, too, are so dazzled by power and money that we forget the fragility of our existence'. 'Everywhere people seek career advancement,' Christopher R. Browning similarly concludes in *Ordinary Men* (1992), his path-breaking study of how people trained to respect authority and the conventional norms of their peers lose their sense of personal responsibility and come to participate in genocidal violence.

In their indifference to career advancement, and their challenge to the establishment either to reform itself or to crush them, the protesters have demonstrated an uncommon kind of courage. Refusing complicity with corrupted institutions, they have expressed a necessary faith in the human capacity to resist thuggish authority and to recognise and empathise with the powerless in any situation. They have dared to take some risks on behalf of freedom, dignity and equality. To the survivalist and bystander mindset that dominates political and professional life today, they have posed a formidable moral challenge with their self-denying acts.

Increasingly, it seems that only those jolted into ethical consciousness by the calamity of Gaza can be trusted to restore the strength and dignity of the individual conscience. For they appear to see more clearly than their well-placed elders, where cowardice, conformity and willed stupidity lead, and how, dazzled by power and money, and motivated by career advancement and social promotion, many of us forget the fragility of our existence. These men and women know that if there is any bumper-sticker lesson to be drawn from the Shoah, it is 'Never Again for Anyone': the slogan of the brave young activists of Jewish Voice for Peace.

It is possible, even likely, that they will lose. Israel, with its survivalist psychosis, is not the 'bitter relic' George Steiner called it – rather, it is the portent of the future of a bankrupt and exhausted world. The full-throated endorsement of Israel by far-right maniacs like Javier Milei of Argentina and Jair Bolsonaro of Brazil and its patronage by Western countries where white nationalists have infected political life speaks of a widening inferno of existential terrors. Encouraged by demagogues, more and more people seem convinced that their nation, race, ethnic community or class will not survive unless ruthless measures are taken. As the climate crisis brings forth a world of barbed-wire borders, walls and apartheid, and cruelty in the name of self-preservation receives singularly wide sanction, most recently in Donald Trump's electoral triumph, Israel will most likely succeed in ethnic-cleansing Gaza, and the West Bank as well.

There is already too much evidence that the arc of the moral universe does not bend towards justice; powerful

men have always made their massacres seem necessary and righteous. It's not at all difficult to imagine a
triumphant conclusion to the Israeli onslaught, or its
retrospective sanitising by historians and journalists as
well as politicians. Recalling how 'the intellectual always
and everywhere has been totally under the sway of
power', Améry admitted 'that is the way history was and
that is the way it is. One had fallen under its wheel and
doffed one's cap when a murderer came along.'

The fear of catastrophic defeat weighs on the minds
of the protesters. They have not changed, and probably
won't change, opinion in a hardened Western mainstream. But then Améry himself, when he addressed the
miserable conscience of his time, was 'not at all speaking with the intention to convince; I just blindly throw
my word onto the scale, whatever it may weigh'. Feeling deceived and abandoned by the free world, he kept
speaking 'in order that the crime become a moral reality
for the criminal, in order that he be swept into the truth
of his atrocity'. Those opposing Israeli acts of savagery,
and the Western propaganda by omission and obfusca-
tion, cannot aim for much more. They risk permanently
embittering their lives with failure. But their expressions
of outrage and feats of solidarity may have somewhat
alleviated the great loneliness of the Palestinians. They
also hold out some hope for the world after Gaza.

Select Bibliography

Many of the books I draw on are mentioned in the main text. I list some more here for further reading.

Achcar, Gilbert, *The Arabs and the Holocaust: The Arab–Israeli War of Narratives* (London, 2010).

Améry, Jean, *At the Mind's Limits: Contemplations by a Survivor on Auschwitz and Its Realities* (New York, 1990).

Anderson, Carol, *Bourgeois Radicals: The NAACP and the Struggle for Colonial Liberation, 1941–1960* (New York, 2015).

Anidjar, Gil, *The Jew, the Arab: A History of the Enemy* (Stanford, 2003).

Anziska, Seth, *Preventing Palestine: A Political History from Camp David to Oslo* (Princeton, 2018).

Appadurai, Arjun, *Fear of Small Numbers: An Essay on the Geography of Anger* (Durham, NC, 2006).

Arendt, Hannah, *Eichmann in Jerusalem: A Report on the Banality of Evil* (New York, 1965).

Aschheim, Steven, *Brothers and Strangers: The East European Jew in German and German Jewish Consciousness, 1800–1923* (Madison, 1982).

Aschheim, Steven, *Culture and Catastrophe: German and Jewish Confrontations with National Socialism and Other Crises* (New York, 1996).

Avineri, Shlomo, *Herzl: Theodor Herzl and the Foundation of the Jewish State* (London, 2014).

Avineri, Shlomo, *The Making of Modern Zionism: The Intellectual Origins of the Jewish State* (New York, 2017).

Baconi, Tareq, *Hamas Contained: The Rise and Pacification of Palestinian Resistance* (Stanford, 2018).

Barghouti, Mourid, *I Saw Ramallah* (London, 2005).

Bartov, Omer, *Murder in Our Midst: The Holocaust, Industrial Killing, and Representation* (Oxford, 1996).

Bartov, Omer, *Mirrors of Destruction: War, Genocide, and Modern Identity* (Oxford, 2000).

Bartov, Omer, *Anatomy of a Genocide: The Life and Death of a Town Called Buczacz* (New York, 2018).

Bauman, Zygmunt, *Modernity and the Holocaust* (Ithaca, NY, 1989).

Bayly, C. A., *The Birth of the Modern World, 1780–1914: Global Connections and Comparisons* (Oxford, 2004).

Beinart, Peter, *The Crisis of Zionism* (New York, 2012).

Berman, Marshall, *All That Is Solid Melts into Air: The Experience of Modernity* (New York, 1988).

Biale, David, *Power and Powerlessness in Jewish History* (New York, 1986).

Birnbaum, Pierre, and Katznelson, Ira (eds), *Paths of Emancipation: Jews, States, and Citizenship* (Princeton, 1995).

Black, Ian, *Enemies and Neighbours: Arabs and Jews in Palestine and Israel, 1917–2017* (London, 2017).

Blackbourn, David, *Germany in the World: A Global History, 1500–2000* (New York, 2023).

Borstelmann, Thomas, *The Cold War and the Color Line: American Race Relations in the Global Arena* (Cambridge, MA, 2003).

Brenner, Michael, *The Renaissance of Jewish Culture in Weimar Germany* (New Haven, 1996).

Brenner, Michael, *In Search of Israel: The History of an Idea* (Princeton, 2018).

Brodkin, Karen, *How Jews Became White Folks and What That Says About Race in America* (New Brunswick, 1998).

Browning, Christopher R., *The Path to Genocide: Essays on Launching the Final Solution* (Cambridge, 1992).

Buber, Martin, *A Land of Two Peoples: Martin Buber on Jews and Arabs*, ed. Paul Mendes-Flohr (Chicago, 2005).

Cesarani, David, *The Jewish Chronicle and Anglo-Jewry, 1841–1991* (Cambridge, 1994).

Cohn, Norman, *Warrant for Genocide: The Myth of the Jewish World-Conspiracy and the Protocols of the Elders of Zion* (Harmondsworth, 1970).

Cooper, Frederick, and Burbank, Jane, *Empires in World History: Power and the Politics of Difference* (Princeton, 2010).

Deák, István, Gross, Jan T., and Judt, Tony (eds), *The Politics of Retribution in Europe: World War II and Its Aftermath* (Princeton, 2000).

Deák, István, *Europe on Trial: The Story of Collaboration, Resistance, and Retribution During World War II* (New York, 2019).

Dirlik, Arif, *The Postcolonial Aura: Third World Criticism in the Age of Global Capitalism* (Boulder, 1997).

Dower, John W., *Ways of Forgetting, Ways of Remembering: Japan in the Modern World* (New York, 2014).

Duara, Prasenjit (ed.), *Decolonization: Perspectives from Now and Then* (New York, 2004).

Dubow, Saul, *Apartheid, 1948–1994* (Oxford, 2014).

Elkins, Caroline, and Pedersen, Susan (eds), *Settler Colonialism in the Twentieth Century: Projects, Practices, Legacies* (New York, 2005).

Elon, Amos, *Herzl* (New York, 1975).

Elon, Amos, *A Blood-Dimmed Tide: Dispatches from the Middle East* (New York, 1997).

Evans, Richard J., *In Hitler's Shadow: West German Historians and the Attempt to Escape from the Nazi Past* (New York, 1989).

Fink, Carole, *West Germany and Israel: Foreign Relations, Domestic Politics, and the Cold War, 1965–1974* (Cambridge, 2019).

Fischbach, Michael R., *Black Power and Palestine: Transnational Countries of Color* (Stanford, 2018).

Franaszek, Andrzej, *Milosz: A Biography* (Cambridge, MA, 2017).

Friedländer, Saul, *When Memory Comes* (New York, 1979).

Friedländer, Saul (ed.), *Probing the Limits of Representation: Nazism and the 'Final Solution'* (Cambridge, MA, 1992).

Fritzsche, Peter, *Reading Berlin: 1900* (Cambridge, MA, 1996).

Garavini, Giuliano, *After Empires: European Integration, Decolonization, and the Challenge from the Global South, 1957–1986* (Oxford, 2012).

Gay, Peter, *Freud, Jews and Other Germans: Masters and Victims in Modernist Culture* (New York, 1978).

Genet, Jean, *Prisoner of Love* (London, 1989).

Getachew, Adom, *Worldmaking After Empire: The Rise and Fall of Self-Determination* (Princeton, 2019).

Gilbert, Shirli, and Alba, Avril (eds), *Holocaust Memory and Racism in the Postwar World* (Detroit, 2019).

Gildea, Robert, *Empires of the Mind: The Colonial Past and the Politics of the Present* (Cambridge, MA, 2019).

Gilman, Sander L., *Jewish Self-Hatred: Anti-Semitism and the Hidden Language of the Jews* (Baltimore, 1986).

Gilroy, Paul, *The Black Atlantic: Modernity and Double Consciousness* (Cambridge, MA, 1993).

Goldstein, Eric L., *The Price of Whiteness: Jews, Race, and American Identity* (Princeton, 2006).

Gordon, Adi, *Toward Nationalism's End: An Intellectual Biography of Hans Kohn* (Waltham, MA, 2017).

Gorenberg, Gershom, *The Accidental Empire: Israel and the Birth of the Settlements, 1967–1977* (New York, 2006).

Greenberg, Udi, *The Weimar Century: German Émigrés and the Ideological Foundations of the Cold War* (Princeton, 2014).

Ha'am, Ahad, *Nationalism and the Jewish Ethic*, ed. and with an introduction by Hans Kohn (New York, 1962).

Halkin, Hillel, *Jabotinsky: A Life* (New Haven, 2014).

Hayes, Peter (ed.), *Lessons and Legacies: The Meaning of the Holocaust in a Changing World* (Evanston, 1991).

Heller, Erich, *The Disinherited Mind* (New York, 1959).

Hertz, Deborah, *How Jews Became Germans: The History of Conversion and Assimilation in Berlin* (New Haven, 2007).

Hertzberg, Arthur, *The Zionist Idea: A Historical Analysis and Reader* (New York, 1959).

Hess, Jonathan, *Germans, Jews and the Claims of Modernity* (New Haven, 2002).

Hoffman, Adina, *My Happiness Bears No Relation to Happiness: A Poet's Life in the Palestinian Century* (New Haven, 2009).

Howe, Irving, *World of Our Fathers* (New York, 1976).

Irwin, Ryan M., *Gordian Knot: Apartheid and the Unmaking of the Liberal World Order* (Oxford, 2012).

Iyad, Abu, with Eric Rouleau, *My Home, My Land: A Narrative of the Palestinian Struggle* (New York, 1981).

Jackson, Patrick Thaddeus, *Civilizing the Enemy: German Reconstruction and the Invention of the West* (Ann Arbor, 2006).

Jansen, Jan C., and Osterhammel, Jürgen, *Decolonization: A Short History* (Princeton, 2017).

Kalmar, Ivan Davidson, and Penslar, Derek J. (eds), *Orientalism and the Jews* (Waltham, MA, 2005).

Kaplan, Marion A., *Between Dignity and Despair: Jewish Life in Nazi Germany* (Oxford, 1998).

Karmi, Ghada, *In Search of Fatima: A Palestinian Story* (London, 2002).

Kathrada, Ahmed, *A Simple Freedom: The Strong Mind of Robben Island Prisoner, No. 468/64* (Johannesburg, 2008).

Kazin, Alfred, *Alfred Kazin's Journals* (New Haven, 2011).

Khalidi, Rashid, *Palestinian Identity: The Construction of Modern National Consciousness* (New York, 1997).

Khalidi, Rashid, *The Iron Cage: The Story of the Palestinian Struggle for Statehood* (Boston, 2006).

Khalili, Laleh, *Time in the Shadows: Confinement in Counterinsurgencies* (Stanford, 2012).

Kohn, Hans, *Living in a World Revolution: My Encounters with History* (New York, 1964).

Krall, Hanna, *Shielding the Flame: An Intimate Conversation with Dr Marek Edelman* (New York, 1986).

Kushner, Tony, *The Holocaust and the Liberal Imagination: A Social and Cultural History* (Oxford, 1994).

LaCapra, Dominick, *Representing the Holocaust: History, Theory, Trauma* (Ithaca, NY, 1994).

Lake, Marilyn, and Reynolds, Henry, *Drawing the Global Colour Line: White Men's Countries and the International Challenge of Racial Equality* (Cambridge, 2008).

Lang, Berel, *The Future of the Holocaust: Between History and Memory* (Ithaca, NY, 1999).

Lang, Berel, *Primo Levi: The Matter of a Life* (New Haven, 2013).

Langbehn, Volker, and Salama, Mohammad, *German Colonialism: Race, the Holocaust, and Postwar Germany* (New York, 2011).

Laqueur, Walter, *A History of Zionism* (London, 1972).

Laron, Guy, *The Six Day War: The Breaking of the Middle East* (New Haven, 2017).

Lee, Christopher J. (ed.), *Making a World After Empire: The Bandung Moment and Its Political Afterlives* (Athens, OH, 2010).

Levi, Primo, *The Voice of Memory: Interviews, 1961–1987* (New York, 2001).

Mamdani, Mahmood, *When Victims Become Killers: Colonialism, Nativism, and the Genocide in Rwanda* (Princeton, 2001).

Mamdani, Mahmood, *Neither Settler nor Native: The Making and Unmaking of Permanent Minorities* (Cambridge, MA, 2020).

Mandel, Maud S., *In the Aftermath of Genocide: Armenians and Jews in Twentieth-Century France* (Durham, NC, 2003).

Marchand, Suzanne L., *German Orientalism in the Age of Empire: Religion, Race and Scholarship* (Cambridge, 2009).

Mazower, Mark, *Hitler's Empire: How the Nazis Ruled Europe* (New York, 2009).

Mendes-Flohr, Paul, *Divided Passions: Jewish Intellectuals and the Experience of Modernity* (Detroit, 1991).

Mikel-Arieli, Roni, *Remembering the Holocaust in a Racial State: Holocaust Memory in South Africa from Apartheid to Democracy (1948–1994)* (Boston, 2022).

Milosz, Czeslaw, *Legends of Modernity: Essays and Letters from Occupied Poland, 1942–1943* (New York, 2006).

Moses, A. Dirk, and Stone, Dan (eds), *Colonialism and Genocide* (New York, 2007).

Mosse, George, *German Jews Beyond Judaism* (Bloomington, 1985).

Mosse, George, *Confronting the Nation: Jewish and Western Nationalism* (Hanover, NH, 1993).

Mosse, George, *The Fascist Revolution: Toward a General Theory of Fascism* (New York, 1999).

Moyn, Samuel, *A Holocaust Controversy: The Treblinka Affair in Postwar France* (Waltham, MA, 2005).

Myers, David N., *Re-Inventing the Jewish Past: European Jewish Intellectuals and the Zionist Return to History* (Oxford, 1995).

Naimark, Norman M., *Fires of Hatred: Ethnic Cleansing in Twentieth-Century Europe* (Cambridge, MA, 2002).

Nathans, Benjamin, *Beyond the Pale: The Jewish Encounter with Late Imperial Russia* (Berkeley, 2002).

Penslar, Derek J., *Israel in History: The Jewish State in Comparative Perspective* (New York, 2007).

Peukert, Detlev J. K., *The Weimar Republic: The Crisis of Classical Modernity* (New York, 1992).

Prashad, Vijay, *The Darker Nations: A People's History of the Third World* (New York, 2007).

Presner, Todd Samuel, *Muscular Judaism: The Jewish Body and the Politics of Regeneration* (New York, 2007).

Pulzer, Peter, *The Rise of Political Anti-Semitism in Germany and Austria* (Cambridge, MA, 1988).

Rabinbach, Anson, *In the Shadow of Catastrophe: German Intellectuals Between Apocalypse and Enlightenment* (Berkeley, 1997).

Reitter, Paul, *On the Origins of Jewish Self-Hatred* (Princeton, 2012).

Reitter, Paul, *Bambi's Jewish Roots and Other Essays on German-Jewish Culture* (New York, 2015).

Rose, Jacqueline, *The Question of Zion* (Princeton, 2005).

Roth, Joseph, *The Wandering Jews* (New York, 2001).

Roth, Joseph, *What I Saw: Reports from Berlin, 1920–1933* (New York, 2003).

Roth, Philip, *Operation Shylock: A Confession* (New York, 1993).

Sands, Philippe, *East West Street: On the Origins of Genocide and Crimes Against Humanity* (London, 2016).

Schwarz, Bill, *The White Man's World* (Oxford, 2011).

Scott, David, *Conscripts of Modernity: The Tragedy of Colonial Enlightenment* (Durham, NC, 2004).

Segev, Tom, *1949: The First Israelis* (New York, 1986).

Segev, Tom, *One Palestine, Complete: Jews and Arabs Under the British Mandate* (New York, 2000).

Shapira, Anita, *Land and Power: The Zionist Resort to Force, 1881–1948* (Oxford, 1992).

Shapira, Anita, *Ben-Gurion: Father of Modern Israel* (New Haven, 2014).

Shehadeh, Raja, *A Rift in Time: Travels with My Ottoman Uncle* (New York, 2011).

Shehadeh, Raja, *Occupation Diaries* (London, 2012).

Shimoni, Gideon, *Jews and Zionism: The South African Experience (1910–1967)* (Cape Town, 1980).

Shimoni, Gideon, *Community and Conscience: The Jews in Apartheid South Africa* (Hanover, NH, 2003).

Shlaim, Avi, *The Iron Wall: Israel and the Arab World* (London, 2000).

Shulman, David, *Dark Hope: Working for Peace in Israel and Palestine* (Chicago, 2007).

Singh, Nikhil Pal, *Climbin' Jacob's Ladder: The Black Freedom Movement Writings of Jack O'Dell* (Berkeley, 2010).

Stanislawski, Michael, *Zionism and the Fin de Siècle: Cosmopolitanism and Nationalism from Nordau to Jabotinsky* (Berkeley, 2001).

Staub, Michael E., *Torn at the Roots: The Crisis of Jewish Liberalism in Postwar America* (New York, 2002).

Steiner, George, *Language and Silence: Essays on Language, Literature, and the Inhuman* (New Haven, 1970).

Stern, Fritz, *Dreams and Delusions: The Drama of German History* (New York, 1987).

Sternhell, Zeev, *The Founding Myths of Israel: Nationalism, Socialism, and the Making of the Jewish State* (Princeton, 1998).

Talmon, Jacob L., *Mission and Testimony: Political Essays* (Eastbourne, 2015).

Taylor, Frederick, *Exorcising Hitler: The Occupation and Denazification of Germany* (London, 2012).

Thomson, Ian, *Primo Levi: A Life* (New York, 2003).

Todorov, Tzvetan, *Facing the Extreme: Moral Life in the Concentration Camps* (New York, 1997).

Veidlinger, Jeffrey, *In the Midst of Civilized Europe: The 1918–1921 Pogroms in Ukraine and the Onset of the Holocaust* (London, 2021).

Vidal-Naquet, Pierre, *Assassins of Memory: Essays on the Denial of the Holocaust* (New York, 1992).

Vidal-Naquet, Pierre, *The Jews: History, Memory, and the Present* (New York, 1998).

Vital, David, *The Origins of Zionism* (Oxford, 1975).

Volkov, Shulamit, *Walther Rathenau: Weimar's Fallen Statesman* (New Haven, 2012).

Wells, Allen, *Tropical Zion: General Trujillo, FDR, and the Jews of Sosúa* (Durham, NC, 2009).

Whitman, James Q., *Hitler's American Model: The United States and the Making of Nazi Race Law* (Princeton, 2017).

Wilder, Gary, *Freedom Time: Negritude, Decolonization, and the Future of the World* (Durham, NC, 2015).

Wright, Richard A., *Black Power, Three Books from Exile: Black Power / The Color Curtain / White Man, Listen!* (New York, 2008).

Zahra, Tara, *The Great Departure: Mass Migration from Eastern Europe and the Making of the Free World* (New York, 2016).

Zertal, Idith, *From Catastrophe to Power: Holocaust Survivors and the Emergence of Israel* (Berkeley, 1998).

Zipperstein, Steven J., *Elusive Prophet: Ahad Ha'am and the Origins of Zionism* (Berkeley, 1993).

Zipperstein, Steven J., *Pogrom: Kishinev and the Tilt of History* (New York, 2018).